HOPE
A Personal Testimony

When It
of How to Deal With

HURTS
the Impact of Cancer

Larry Burkett

With Michael E. Taylor

HOPE

A Personal Testimony

When It

of How to Deal With

HURTS

the Impact of Cancer

MOODY PRESS
CHICAGO

About the Author

LARRY BURKETT is founder and president of Christian Financial Concepts, a nonprofit ministry that teaches biblical principles of finance and trains others to counsel and teach using these principles. Larry holds degrees in marketing and finance, as well as an Honorary Doctorate in economics. He hosts two radio programs, heard on 1,100 radio outlets, and has written more than fifty books, which include the best-sellers *The Coming Economic Earthquake, Debt-Free Living, Women Leaving the Workplace,* and *The Financial Planning Workbook.* Larry and Judy live in Gainesville, Georgia and have four children and nine grandchildren.

Travis Massey
Magic Craft Studio

Contents

Acknowledgments

I would like to express my appreciation to Adeline Griffith and Mike Taylor. Without them this book would not have been written.

I also appreciate Drs. Lee Cowden, Dan Clark, and Nick Martin for their willingness to share their evaluations of our current medical system.

And I thank all of those who have prayed (and are praying) for my health during this most trying period of my life. Truly God hears the prayers of His people.

Prologue

In the years since I was diagnosed with cancer, I can honestly say that God has been good to me. He hasn't chosen to rescue me from this difficulty but, rather, has sustained me through it.

I have never asked God *why* this happened. It really doesn't matter *why*. Instead, I have asked *what* God would have me to do as a result of having cancer. I believe this book is a direct result of asking God what I should do. I have tried to be totally (some say brutally) honest about my feelings and my doubts since the beginning.

We are not supernatural beings; only God is. We are human beings and, as such, we have all the normal human emotions that

God equipped us with—that includes me. But under the influence of the Holy Spirit we can learn to control those emotions,
even overcome them. The fact is, cancer is a very serious disease.
God could supernaturally heal me. I know that. But at this time
He has not chosen to do so. Instead, God has chosen to give me
His supernatural peace about this whole process. If there is a
choice, I'll take the peace of God every time.

We're all going to die some day; that is *not* a choice. We can
choose to live in fear, or anger, or pity, or in the peace of God;
that's *our* choice. I choose to live in God's peace, enjoying each
and every day as best I can. I sincerely pray that all of God's people will choose to do the same. Happiness *really* is a choice.

I have received thousands of letters from Christians who have
been diagnosed with cancer but refuse to accept it. Many are very
fearful of dying and, thus, believe if they deny the reality of their
illness it will go away. Others refuse treatment because they think
that to accept man's medicine is to reject God's healing.

It is my personal conviction that we need *facts* in order to make
good decisions. Denial in the face of cancer brings almost certain
death. Furthermore, God's healing is *His* choice and I personally
believe that if God decides to heal me miraculously it really won't
matter what other alternatives I might be pursuing at the time.

Remember God *spoke* this entire physical universe into existence; therefore, I suspect He can handle our puny problems whenever He wants to.

It has now been more than three years since I was diagnosed
with metastatic renal cell carcinoma. Depending on whose statistics you read, I have survived well beyond the odds for this disease. Best of all, I feel very well! Other than the nagging residual
pain from my two major surgeries, which is to be expected, I am
as active as ever.

I continue to take an immune boosting compound from the
Aliatros group, Prague, Czech Republic. The use of this treatment
(called AM-2) has now been approved in the U.S. and is available

in many locations. The contact information is located in the reference section.

The effect of this all-natural compound continues to be verified through better immune system tests that have been developed recently. One test (labeled IL-8) monitors the overall ability of the immune system to fight diseases. The "normal" range for healthy adults is 30 to 70. Many patients receiving the AM-2 treatments show an IL-8 score of more than 2,000! That's impressive enough to convince me to recommend it to others.

There are many exciting new therapies being tested throughout the world, including the United States. I heard about one such treatment being offered at the West Clinic in Memphis, Tennessee and applied for acceptance into the test program. My minimum criteria for any therapy is (1) It must have scientific credibility—no chicken bones or chants; (2) It has to be shown effective for my particular type of cancer (renal cell); and (3) It must be reasonably affordable (since experimental therapies are not covered by health insurance). This treatment, known as autolymphocyte therapy (ALT), meets those criteria.

ALT consists of removing some of my white blood cells, stimulating them ex-vivos (externally) with a powerful immune modulator, and reinfusing them into my blood seven days later. This effectively "supercharges" my natural defense system and, thus, helps to reduce the probability of a reoccurrence. This therapy should be very effective against other types of cancer also. However, due to current FDA rules, it is not available for other types of cancer.

Somehow, that doesn't make a lot of sense to me. If someone has a life-threatening disease like cancer and is willing to take personal responsibility for any treatment, it should be that person's choice, not some government agency's. It's amazing that our laws allow a 13 year-old girl to have an abortion but prohibit a 65 year-old cancer patient from having a treatment being administered by licensed physicians in hospitals. That is just plain NUTS!

In 1997 I helped to get the laws in Georgia changed to allow our doctors to prescribe and administer any known treatment to their patients, provided the potential risks of the treatments are clearly explained in advance. Georgia joins at least seven other states that have passed similar laws. Unfortunately, the powerful influence of the federal laws still overshadow this area. Basically it boils down to the fact that if a company wants their treatment approved by the FDA, and thus allowed by the insurance companies, they must play by the FDA's rules.

I am convinced that eventually the Congress will act on the behalf of millions of cancer patients who have exhausted all the known treatments for their diseases. It is criminal to tell these people that it's better for them to *die* than to risk an experimental treatment that might *harm* them. If you feel the same way, contact your senators and representatives in Congress and let them know how you feel.

There are many exciting breakthroughs in cancer therapy being developed, including gene splicing therapies, enzyme inhibitors that choke off the blood supply to the tumors, genes that trigger the cancer cells to die, and dozens more. Scientists have proved that these therapies can kill cancer in test animals; now we need the right to test them in suffering human beings. Under current laws it will be ten years or more before these new therapies can be brought to the public. That's unacceptable.

Please understand that I head a financial ministry—not a cancer research organization. It's extremely difficult for my staff to respond to cancer information inquiries. Instead, I suggest that you locate some of the resource books listed in the Appendix.

The Internet is also an excellent resource. Through the World Wide Web, virtually all the resources of the world are available to you. If you can't find these resources yourself, let your church know. God has placed knowledgeable Christians everywhere. There is most certainly someone who will help you if you let the need be known.

Until we meet . . .

April 1998

Introduction

Following God's prompting, in 1976 I started the ministry known today as Christian Financial Concepts, for the purpose of teaching biblical principles of money management to God's people. The heart of my message has always been that we're stewards, and not owners, of all that God entrusts to us. Although most people think of money management when they hear the word *stewardship*, the principle actually has a broader application and includes the use of our God-given talents, our knowledge of the Gospel, and even the bodies that we inhabit while living on this earth.

Being a steward of these areas means that we receive what God has given us, and we use everything to His glory, in order to minister to others. Rather than being only a recipient of blessings, God's plan is for us to be a purveyor of blessings to others, and these blessings flow in the bad times as well as in the good.

A new chapter on obedience in my life began in March of 1995, with the discovery of two malignant tumors in my body. In retrospect, there were two biblical passages that were foundational to my thoughts. *"Trust in the Lord with all your heart, and do not lean on your own understanding. In all your ways acknowledge Him, and He will make your paths straight"* (Proverbs 3:5–6). And, *"Let a man regard us in this manner, as servants of Christ, and stewards of the mysteries of God. In this case, moreover, it is required of stewards that one be found trustworthy"* (1 Corinthians 4:1–2).

The verses from Proverbs are self-explanatory. We are to trust in God even when our own understanding fails us (or perhaps *especially* when our understanding fails us).

Three elements from the Corinthians passage stand out to me: *servants of Christ, stewards of the mysteries of God,* and *trustworthy.* It is my heart's desire to continue to serve Christ here on this earth. Perhaps the Lord will be gracious to me and grant another fifteen years to my life like He did King Hezekiah (see 2 Kings 20:1–6); I don't know. But I do have work I'd like to continue. However, as Christ prayed to the Father, *"Yet not as I will, but as Thou wilt."*

I also believe we're stewards of the mysteries of God. By mysteries, I mean things that are not immediately evident about God, in the human sense, which we learn primarily through difficult times. I used to think I knew a little about pain and suffering. I also believed I could face death without fear.

I have known the Lord personally for some twenty-six years. During that time I have discovered that as far as knowing what you *really* believe there is no substitute for looking death squarely in the face. Then we find out what caliber of Christian we are and if we're ready to meet our Savior face-to-face.

Through my cancer experience, Christ has taught me new things about Himself—mysteries, if you will. I don't want to hide what I have learned under a bushel. If you can benefit from my experiences, so be it. One thing you will learn as you read this book is that I believe in sharing the undiluted truth. I am who I am, and I can't pretend to be something I'm not. And one thing I'm not is perfect.

Throughout this ordeal, God has been my anchor, my peace, and my security. But His blessings are not mine to hide. In an effort to be a good steward, I want to pass on to you the things I have experienced, the feelings I have felt, the insights I have gained into both Scripture and in my relationship with God, and some overall reflections on medical treatment here in the United States.

Above all else, it is my desire for the Lord Jesus to count me *trustworthy* with the work He has given me to do here on earth. At this point in time, I believe that work includes telling this story. According to 2 Corinthians 5:10, one day I will personally stand before Him, and I don't want to hear Him say to me, "Larry, I hoped I could count on you for this or that, but you just weren't dependable. I had to work through someone else." No way.

Until the day I draw my last breath, my mission is to be trustworthy with the work He has given me to do. I want to hear my Master say, *"Well done, good and faithful slave; you were faithful with a few things, I will put you in charge of many things, enter into the joy of your master"* (Matthew 25:21).

I want to reach several specific groups with the message of this book.

1. People who are presently dealing with cancer and other life-threatening diseases, including those in various stages of remission.

Following my surgeries, I have found that the coping process is far more than just physical. It is, first of all, spiritual, then emotional, then mental; and I have some thoughtful insights to share with those of you who are struggling in these areas.

But I have another message to share with those coping with afflictions, especially cancer. When my doctors said that there really wasn't any treatment other than surgery to offer me, I discovered how difficult it was to obtain information on alternative treatments for cancer. My daughter Kim spent hours researching possibilities for me, and one of the goals of this book is to centralize some resources for what are called nontraditional therapies for combating cancer.

Many of the alternative treatments we investigated were easily dismissed as quackery. But, some weren't, and here's the key. Don't overlook the legitimate alternative therapies that really *can* help you because of the other pseudo-medical fakes. To help me sort out what constitutes legitimate alternative therapies, we settled on a system that will be explained later in the book.

2. Families who have a loved one with cancer.

With so much focus on the well-being of the cancer patient, frequently the needs of the family get overlooked. I've asked my wife Judy, who most closely shared this experience with me, to reflect on how she coped with her stress and to pass on some helpful hints for how you can take care of yourself, as well as the cancer patient. Because of high levels of stress and worry, I have found that it is easy for a family's support system to burn out and collapse. Judy will offer some ideas in chapter 8 on how to prevent that from happening to you.

3. Christians within the medical professions.

I will acknowledge up front that I am a newcomer to the field of cancer treatment, and my personal experience does not make me a trained professional. Yet, sometimes there can be fresh, objective insights from someone removed from the daily routines and mind-set of the establishment.

Overall, there are some wonderful, compassionate people in the medical professions, and it has been my blessing from God to receive their services. There also are others who are set in their ways and not only refuse to acknowledge that there are some potentially beneficial therapies outside the U.S. but they, in fact, actively try to block all knowledge of them. There is good and bad on both sides and, in truth, some aspects of current cancer treatment in the U.S. are quite harmful to your health.

4. *People who are suffering.*

In a broader sense, the insights and principles I hope to offer will be applicable to nearly anyone dealing with sickness and suffering—any who are seeking to synthesize their Christian faith with their experience. I have found a great deal of convoluted, unbiblical theology floating around that causes Christians additional emotional, mental, and spiritual suffering; and this should be corrected. After all, it's enough just to deal with the physical problems without having to deal with destructive doctrines as well.

5. *Members of the body of Christ.*

In this book, I plan to share some personal experiences and insights that illustrate how the body of Christ can be helpful when ministering to people with cancer or who are otherwise dealing with suffering. Dealing with a potentially terminal illness can lead to awkward social relationships; few people, even in the church, know how to talk about death. While facing this crisis, I met some well-intentioned people who, without meaning to, really discouraged me by what they said and did. Some people were so thoughtless it's hard to believe.

On the other hand, I have had some beautiful words of encouragement from the body of Christ, many of which came in the thousands of cards and letters mailed to us after it was discovered that I had cancer. I'll share some of that correspondence with you, along with some hints about how you and your church family can be helpful to someone with cancer or other serious illnesses.

Finally, I want to share with you the greatest promise ever made: the promise of eternal life. The apostle John wrote, *"These have been written that you may believe that Jesus is the Christ, the Son of God; and that believing you may have life in His name"* (John 20:31).

In reality, we're all terminally ill with a condition called sin. The Bible says in Hebrews 9:27, *"It is appointed for men to die once and after this comes judgment."* My particular affliction is called cancer; yours may have another name. But the fact is that every living and breathing person on earth is dying and needs a savior, and the Bible reveals that only Jesus Christ is worthy of your trust.

If you're fighting a serious illness, the important thing to remember is that *we will all die some day.* Death is inevitable. Life with Christ is everlasting. God gave us remarkable bodies that are capable of self-healing if we treat them properly. But a hundred years from now, we all will have died. Then the only thing that will matter is our individual relationship with Jesus Christ, the Savior.

My deepest prayer is that you will find complete peace and rest with our Lord as a result of reading this book.

Larry Burkett

June 1996

CHAPTER ONE

My New Golf Handicap: An Aching Shoulder!

S ometimes God has strange ways of leading people. He showed the way to Moses and the Israelites with a pillar of cloud by day and a pillar of fire by night. God showed Jonah the directions to Nineveh, via a whale. God captured Balaam's attention by speaking through a donkey. The apostles drew lots to select Matthias as the replacement for Judas.

So maybe it's not so unusual for me to say that God provided a major leading in my life through the game of *golf*. Imagine that: The pastime that causes so many to compromise their religious convictions for a Sunday morning game was used by God in a way that may have extended my life here on earth. Here's how it happened.

Because of some eyesight problems, I had to give up playing tennis, and golf seemed like a suitable new challenge, especially since all my brothers played. I started playing golf in 1992, and for the first year or so I spent more time practicing than anything else. Almost from the beginning I can remember experiencing pain and tenderness in my left shoulder. I figured pain was a natural consequence of growing older, and since I was in my early 50s I didn't think much about it.

By the spring of 1994 I had improved, so I decided to take some lessons at a nearby driving range. During my first lesson, in order to check my swing and offer suggestions for improvement, the instructor had me hit about 400 golf balls. My left shoulder hurt so badly afterward that I couldn't use my arm at all the next day. Thinking I had pulled a muscle, I avoided any further use of it, and within a couple of days it was as good as new.

So I headed back to the driving range the next week, ready for another set of lessons. But the second lesson was cut short after hitting about 100 balls because the pain became too intense. By intense I mean that when I began concentrating more on avoiding the pain than on consistency in my swing, I just quit. I knew something was wrong, and I knew it wasn't old age.

A visit to an orthopedist resulted in several possibilities: I could have bursitis, arthritis, or perhaps even a torn rotator-cuff in my left shoulder, he said. To pin down the exact problem would require an extensive set of tests. Instead, I decided, *If it's bursitis or arthritis, I can take something like Motrin, and it'll probably go away.*

It did. Within days, I was feeling good as new again. That lasted until the next time I played golf, which happened to be with my stepfather on a course in North Carolina. I stepped to the number one tee, eager to really crunch my first tee shot—John Daly style. When I swung, however, I simultaneously felt and heard something "pop" in my shoulder, and I was in immediate agony. There was no way I could lift a club, much less swing it another time. The searing pain was ten times worse than it had ever been, and I can only describe it as the sensation of a raging fire in one of my joints.

That event led to a series of visits to several doctors over the next nine months in the attempt to discover the source of my shoulder pain. One thought it could be a bone spur, presumably a nagging carryover from a broken collarbone, from my high school football days. Another concluded that it was little more than bursitis or arthritis. My golfing buddies joked and told me to quit making excuses for my game. I really didn't know what to think.

At the suggestion of a doctor friend at Emory University Hospital, I was examined by an orthopedist who regularly caters to professional athletes in the Atlanta area. He spent an entire hour bending, twisting, and poking my left shoulder.

"There," he said, after injecting a localized anesthetic. "Does that help your shoulder?" I moved my arm around a little bit. "No, it hurts like always," I replied.

"Then you don't have a shoulder problem, my friend," he said with finality. "If you did, that would have helped." God provided a timely insight through this man, and I appreciated his skill and expertise.

He decided that I needed to get an MRI on the whole shoulder area. Doing so would expand the area of search by several inches or so. An MRI, or magnetic resonance imaging, is done on a machine that uses magnetic lines of flux to detail the inside of your body. As you lie completely still on a backboard, the technicians slide you inside a tube, with your nose about two inches from the roof. That makes for claustrophobia, and most patients require some degree of medication to tolerate it. So did I.

On Friday, March 10, I slipped out of the CFC offices in Gainesville, Georgia, and went to a local imaging center to get an MRI on my shoulder. Frankly, I had been in and out of so many doctors' offices over the last three years that my hopes for an answer were rapidly diminishing. Little did I know that this test would get to the root of my problem.

When the test was completed, the MRI technician said, "Thanks, Mr. Burkett. The doctor will call you the first of the week, after he has studied your results."

Leaving the medical center, I swung by home to pick up my wife Judy and we scooted out of town, driving to our retreat in North Carolina for the weekend. My schedule had been hectic of late, and I needed a break. After a relaxing weekend in the mountains, during the next week, I planned to knock out the last three chapters of a book I was writing for Moody Press.

A MASS? WHAT'S A MASS?

The phone rang in our North Carolina cabin early that Monday, startling me with its irritating noise. It broke my concentration. I quickly finished the last words of the sentence I was typing. The second ring raised my ire a little bit. After all, Judy and I had gone to the cabin to get away from the phone.

As I stretched to answer the call on Monday morning, March 13, 1995, I had no idea just how dramatic this interruption would be. My life was about to change in a big way.

The caller was the doctor from the Imaging Center in Gainesville, where I had the MRI scan on my ailing shoulder the previous Friday. He got right to the point.

"Larry, I reviewed your MRI first thing this morning and I'm troubled. You have a mass in your left shoulder. You need to get back here right now."

I was stunned. Even though he said "mass," I immediately thought "cancer." Sure, I'd had problems with my shoulder for the past two years, but cancer never even crossed my mind. There never had been cancer in my family, on either my mother's or father's side, for as far back as anybody can remember. In fact, the Burkett males usually died of heart attacks; it's kind of a family tradition. But cancer? Never. The news was a complete shock.

The doctor went on to explain that the mass might not be cancer; it could simply be a benign growth. "Some tumors are harmless," he said, "but let's not take a chance. I want you to come back right away." I hung up the phone and tried to gather my thoughts. Shortly after the phone call, Judy returned from a near-by grocery store. As she placed the plastic grocery bags on the counter, I called for her to join me. "Honey, sit down a minute. I have something to tell you."

In 1978 Judy and I purchased my mother's cottage in Waynesville, North Carolina. It serves as a wonderful getaway, where I can be refreshed, soak in some solitude, and have focused time in God's Word. If you're like me, sometimes you need to get away just to have time to think. Perhaps we're so busy these days we don't have enough time to sit back and ponder things.

Those of you who write will appreciate the need to cultivate creativity by scheduling time to be quiet, meditate, and clarify your thoughts. I'm that way too. I can't force creativity. Rather, I find that in order to be creative I have to get to an environment that is free from distractions and conducive to writing. The cottage tucked away in the Smoky Mountains was the perfect getaway.

Judy and I had driven up to our hideaway the previous Friday evening, and my intent was to finish writing the book *Women Leaving the Workplace,* to be published by Moody Press. I had about three or four chapters to complete, and I began writing early that Monday morning: eager, focused, and ready to get some serious work done.

The news of the phone call hit me like a laser-guided bomb—right in the center of my being.

Outside, the morning sunshine was breaking through the towering pines and the bare oak trees. As usual, several sparrows whisked from tree to tree, chirping at the squirrels, who were trying to raid their feeder. I'm sure that everything outside was normal—just like any other day. But after that phone call I didn't notice.

I told Judy what the radiologist had said. She was as shocked as I had been. "There has to be some mistake," she countered, without much conviction in her voice.

"Maybe," I agreed, hoping to ease her mind, "but we need to head back home."

Judy and I quickly packed our belongings, locked up the cabin, and headed back to north Georgia, not knowing what the future held.

The trip back from North Carolina was mixed with periods of intense conversation between Judy and me, followed by long periods of silence, as each of us tried to take in the news.

"How big of a mass did he say it was?" she asked.

I explained to her that I didn't know; it didn't occur to me to ask at the time. All I really heard the doctor say was that I had a mass and that I needed to get back home as soon as possible.

"What does he mean, 'a mass'?" Judy asked after a long silence. "Does he think it's malignant?"

"He said he didn't know," I replied.

I learned later that doctors don't like to use the word cancer. They say mass or tumor instead. I guess that's supposed to sound better. Maybe it does, unless it's you they're talking about.

"Well, what will they do next?" Judy persisted.

"I don't know. I didn't ask. He just said 'get back,' and that was about all I could handle. My mind was on overload."

BUT WE'VE NEVER HAD CANCER IN OUR FAMILY!

Part of my confusion was due to the fact that, prior to the age of 50, I had been a very healthy person. Then, when I turned 50, I went through a period when my body became weakened from the stress load I was under and, as a result, I caught colds and the flu easily. Then sometime between January and June of 1990, I had an apparent silent heart attack. Then within a year, other problems surfaced.

One was a relatively uncommon form of glaucoma known as pigmentary glaucoma. This condition is caused by the lens of the eyes rubbing up against the pupils, thereby liberating pigment. The condition resulted in partial loss of my peripheral vision. Unfortunately, because of that, I had to give up playing tennis.

Later my glaucoma stabilized, saving my sight. I was relieved, and accepted this condition as something God had allowed in my life. After all, I was getting older, and I assumed that an aging body was going to have some problems from time to time.

But the silent heart attack had proved to be more serious. At first I thought I had the flu, and you know how that goes with us type "A"s. You do the best you can and keep going. If you're committed to your work, as I am, you don't want to wimp out. After several weeks passed and I didn't feel a whole lot better, I decided to get a physical. When a man gets a physical at age 50, one of the first tests the doctors run is a stress EKG, or an electrocardiogram. Basically, they hooked me up to a machine like a treadmill and monitored my heart.

I hadn't walked thirty seconds when the cardiologist exclaimed, "Why didn't you tell me you had a lower branch bundle block?" I didn't have a clue what he was talking about. He continued, "Have you ever been diagnosed with a bundle block before?"

"Not to my knowledge," I replied. "I've passed every test I've ever been given."

"Then get off the machine right now," he ordered as he shut it down. "You've either had a heart attack, or you're having one right now!" He had my full attention. I stopped walking immediately.

Although that was a shock, it was not a surprise. Like I said, heart attacks seem to be a Burkett family tradition. It turns out that the lower branch bundle block meant that I had some nerves in the lower part of my heart that were no longer functioning. All in all, however, I was able to cope very well. I knew a lot about heart trouble. Two of my older brothers had already had heart attacks. In the back of my mind, I guess I was prepared to have trouble also. I just didn't know when.

As a result of further evaluation at Emory University Hospital, I had an angioplasty, which successfully cleared a blockage in one of the lower arteries leading to my heart.

Both of my "major" health problems to date were treatable with moderate medication and an altered lifestyle. Actually, I have since learned that I was too drastic in my attempts to lower my cholesterol. When my heart doctors found that my overall cholesterol was 235, they encouraged me to watch my diet and bring the level down.

I'm the kind of person who likes to see results—quickly! Since I didn't know much about how to treat cholesterol, I made a beeline to a bookstore to pick up some reading material. As I scoured the bookshelves, my eyes latched on a book called *The Eight Week Cholesterol Cure*. I said to myself, *Ah-hah, that's the one for me. A quick cure, that's what I want.*

It was simple. I just followed the diet in the book, which basically consisted of a low-fat, high-fiber diet, combined with high doses of niacin to help lower cholesterol. It worked for me. Within six weeks, I had lowered my cholesterol from 235 to 150. However, there is no doubt that I sometimes suffer from the adage: "If a little is good, a lot is better." So, I doubled the dose of niacin, stopped eating any fats, and dropped my cholesterol below 100. Not good! I know now that too much cholesterol is bad for your body, but too little also can be harmful.

That may have contributed to my problem with the cancer. I don't know for sure, but some articles I have read over the last year indicate that having too low a cholesterol inhibits the body's immune system.

The bottom line is, although I had some previous health troubles, they were always manageable. There was always a treatment I could take or some adjustment I could make that would correct the problem.

But cancer—that's another story. You can diet or exercise as much as you want and still get cancer. There's still a great deal about cancer that doctors don't understand. It's one of a growing list of diseases that continues to elude medical science.

But, back to the tumor-in-the-shoulder problem.

When Judy and I arrived back in Gainesville, it was too late to talk to any doctors. I was scheduled to see a doctor in Atlanta the following Wednesday. All we could do was wait. . .and think. That Monday evening was a very tense time in our home as we tried to get a grip on reality.

PRINCIPLES TO CUSHION THE SHOCK

If you or someone you love has just received some traumatic news, let me encourage you to draw upon the following truths to help cushion the shock.

1. God provides the grace we need in the hour we need it and He will provide for you too.

I've been through a lot since that phone call last year. I've hurt in parts of my body I didn't know could hurt. There were times when I felt overwhelmed and out of control. There were times when I couldn't fathom how I would make it through the next five minutes, much less through the day. Yet in spite of it all, I have found God to be faithful to me. He has never deserted me. By His grace I have managed not only to survive but to grow in Him. God has taught me newer, deeper insights about Him through my suffering. And He has faithfully met my needs.

So the bottom line is to *trust God in our times of need.* God does not promise to meet all of our needs *before* we have them; rather, He promises to provide *when* we have needs.

"Let us therefore draw near with confidence to the throne of grace, that we may receive mercy and may find grace to help in time of need" (Hebrews 4:16).

2. You can be quite mature in your faith and still experience doubts—even depression.

I've served the Lord for over twenty-five years and, yet, the news that I had a tumor struck me to the core of my being. I don't care who you are, when you come face-to-face with death, it takes time simply to grasp the stark reality of your mortality.

I say this because sometimes Christians believe that if they're mature in the Lord, they're not going to experience alarm, or fear, or shock. Those feelings are all natural human emotions. There are still others who truly believe that if they're mature Christians and trusting in the Lord they will never experience *any* difficulties in their lives. Unfortunately, when these people do encounter difficulties, and more specifically crises like cancer, their faith sometimes falls apart.

God does indeed promise that He will love and care for us, but He does not in any way promise to keep us from all the harms of this world. After all, we are mortal beings, living in a sin-fallen world. It may well be that God will elect to reach down and touch an individual and keep him or her from all harm, but I have long since concluded that if God didn't do it for His own apostles, very likely He might not do it for me.

God may allow any one of us to go through some pain, some suffering, even some doubts and fears, in order to mature and use us in His greater plan for this world. That's for God to decide, not us. The inability to accept God's will, to allow Him to use us, can become a wedge between a believer and God. Don't fall into this trap.

Even if you're genuinely committed to Christ, you likely will experience some shock following tragic news. That's completely normal, and feelings of panic do not mean that God has abandoned you. The apostle Paul experienced some doubts and, I think, even fears during his ministry with the Lord. It's very clear that He went through some down times when ministering to the Corinthians, particularly when they abandoned him. But through it all, Paul kept his faith and, as we see in Romans 8, his sense of purpose and, above all, peace.

"Who shall separate us from the love of Christ? Shall tribulation, or distress, or persecution, or famine, or nakedness, or peril, or sword? . . . But in all these things we overwhelmingly conquer through Him who loved us. For I am convinced that neither death, nor life, nor angels, nor principalities, nor things present, nor things to come, nor powers,

nor height, nor depth, nor any other created thing, shall be able to sep-arate us from the love of God, which is in Jesus Christ our Lord" (Romans 8:35, 37–39).

Nothing, including cancer or any other terminal illness—no created thing—can separate you from His strong arms. *Nothing.*

3. Lean on your support system.

Call your family and friends together. Talk to them, pray with them, and let them pray with you. Let your pastor and church leaders know what you're up against. Words simply fail me when I try to communicate what it meant to have my family and friends beside me. We talked, we prayed, we cried, and there were times when we laughed together.

Sometimes a serious or terminal illness provides a focal point, or a rallying point, for people to say things they have thought or felt for years but just never took the time to verbalize. Don't let these precious opportunities pass you by. If you need to express your love, do it. If you need to forgive someone, take care of it. If you have a blessing to pass on to a child or grandchild, do it. Life is too short to let golden opportunities slip by.

Here's the way the apostle James put it. *"Come now, you who say, 'Today or tomorrow, we shall go to such and such a city, and spend a year there and engage in business and make a profit.' Yet you do not know what your life will be like tomorrow. You are just a vapor that appears for a little while and then vanishes away"* (James 4:13–14).

4. Having courage doesn't imply the absence of fear; rather, having courage means facing your fears head-on and over-coming them.

There were times when I was afraid. That doesn't mean I abandoned my faith or didn't trust God. I trusted God and still felt fear. Perhaps it was the fear of the unknown. Usually the things we fear are those things that haven't happened yet. Almost all of us are able to cope with the present, no matter how good or how bad it might be. I recall what Franklin Roosevelt once said, "The only thing we have to fear is fear itself." I believe that's basically true.

Joshua probably felt some fear when God called him to lead the Israelites across the Jordan River into the Promised Land. After all, it would have been so much easier if Moses had finished what he started. And I expect Joshua had keen memories of his earlier excursion into Canaan when he and eleven others spotted giants in the land. Remember the report from the ten spies: *"We became like grasshoppers in our own sight, and so we were in their sight"* (Numbers 13:33).

I personally believe Joshua's heart was pounding in his chest (maybe like yours does when you step into the examination room to hear the results of your tests) as he took the first steps into the Jordan River. God knew all along what Joshua was feeling. Listen to His instruction to His servant. *"Just as I have been with Moses, I will be with you; I will not fail you or forsake you. . . .Have I not commanded you? Be strong and courageous! Do not tremble or be dismayed, for the Lord your God is with you wherever you go"* (Joshua 1:5,9).

Courage is not the absence of fear. Courage is the ability to look fear in the face and proceed with your life.

5. Look for God's peace in the midst of your turmoil.

One of my favorite Bible stories comes from Mark 4:35–41. The passage tells of a fierce storm raging over the Sea of Galilee, threatening to capsize the disciples' little fishing boat. Fearing for their lives, the disciples scrambled to awaken Jesus, who amazingly was sound asleep. *"Teacher, do you not care that we are perishing?"*

I love the way verse 39 reads: *"Being aroused, he rebuked the wind and said to the sea, 'Hush, be still.' And the wind died down and it became perfectly calm."*

That's the Jesus I know. When the emotional storms raged in my heart, I prayed to Him with words similar to the disciples': "Lord, don't you care what's happening?" He did, and He blessed me with His peace—not at first, but soon enough.

He spoke, and the storms within my heart quieted down. This didn't happen all at once, though. Like Peter, I had the peace when I stepped out on the waters, but as the waves began to chop around my feet, I tended to doubt and I questioned God. But like always, Christ was faithful and provided what I asked for—not immediately and not without condition. In large part, the peace of Christ that passes all understanding is also dependent on my ability to let Him provide that peace.

In my case, I realized the answers to my prayers a day at a time and I find that I do the same thing even today. It is interesting, though, that as the news of my condition grew worse, my peace grew stronger. When I felt most out of control, Jesus showed just how *in control* He was.

The word in the Bible to describe what I'm saying is sovereign. My testimony to you is that God is in control. He is holy. He is righteous. He is completely *sovereign*, He never makes a mistake, and He is completely worthy of your trust.

To receive a blessing from the Lord in your time of need, I point you to John 14:27, John 16:33, and Philippians 4:4–7.

Please understand. I'm sharing these insights in retrospect, nearly a year after the doctors discovered my cancer. I have a luxury you may not have at the moment; I've had a year to sort out my experience and feelings. Nonetheless, these are key principles that served as spiritual "anchors" for my soul. I trust they will for you too.

Let's move on to my next major event: my visit to the oncologist/orthopedist.

CHAPTER TWO

❖

I Suspect Another Tumor

Wednesday morning came quickly and, along with it, a trip to see Dr. David Monsen, the renowned orthopedic oncologist at Emory University Hospital in Atlanta. I was anxious to get some answers about the mass growing in my shoulder. My wife Judy, my daughter Kim, and my grandson Ryan accompanied me on the trip. After battling the Atlanta rush hour traffic and finally finding a parking space, we hurried through the maze of halls and corridors and, on several occasions, stopped to ask directions to Dr. Monsen's office.

I don't know if you're like I am, but I don't particularly like hospitals—the smell of hospitals, or even doctor's offices located within the hospital, as Dr. Monsen's was. When we finally arrived, we entered the waiting room, I took a seat, and Judy went over to the receptionist's window to register us.

As I sat there I thought of the number of times I had been to Emory hospital's outpatient cardiology department to have EKGs or stress tests. During those visits, I had glanced over at the wall that said "Oncology Department" on more than one occasion and thought to myself how fortunate I was that I was just going to cardiology rather than oncology.

And now, here I am, I thought to myself. I looked around the room at the other people who were there and quickly decided that I probably didn't fit in. Many of these people looked as if they were ill: thin, emaciated bodies; thinning hair; black eyes—all the chronic and typical symptoms that I envisioned cancer patients would have. *But I'm in good health!* I was walking five miles a day. I was eating well and sleeping well. *So, why am I here?* It didn't make any sense.

Nonetheless, I knew how fortunate I was to have gotten an appointment with Dr. Monsen because he's an extremely busy doctor and considered to be one of the best in his field. Had it not been for a friend of mine who worked at the hospital, who called the doctor personally, I might have had to wait several days before I could get in. But because I didn't have an appointment, I was what they called a "work-in." I understood they would fit me into the schedule when they could.

It turns out there was no need for us to hurry. Although we had arrived early that morning, several hours passed and we were still waiting to be called. Patient after patient was called back to the examination rooms. I flipped through the well-worn magazines. It felt like an eternity. Eventually I heard my name called, and Judy and I were led down the hall to the doctor's office. The nameplate on the door read, DR. DAVID MONSEN.

I entered a well-kept office, which I suspect is unusual for doctors; usually you find things spread out all over the place. But by the looks of the office, I gathered that this doctor was an organized, neat person. I began to glance around the walls at various credentials that he held and the awards that he'd been given and I realized, again, that I was in the hands of one of the best doctors available to me. I was able to relax a little more.

Shortly thereafter, Dr. Monsen came in holding up several of the X rays that had accompanied my MRI, and he pointed out to me that I had a tumor in my left shoulder, probably in the range of three to four centimeters. Then he said something else I wasn't prepared to hear.

"Mr. Burkett, you should realize that a tumor almost never begins in the shoulder. I suspect that you have another tumor somewhere else, so I've ordered some more tests for you. I want you to go through those tests today and then we'll meet again this afternoon to discuss the results."

I was shaken for the second time. I not only faced the prospect of dealing with a tumor in my left shoulder but possibly another tumor somewhere else. And Dr. Monsen's demeanor said it all: *A second tumor will prove this is a malignancy.* Judy and I looked at one another in disbelief. This was much worse than either of us had expected.

Within an hour, I found myself being hustled between the computerized axial tomography machine (CAT scan) and another machine that did a bone scan. I drank some foul-tasting stuff while heading toward one machine and then more foul-tasting stuff as I headed toward the other machine. Little did I know, the outcome of the tests would determine whether I lived or died—and perhaps even how long I would live. It was all happening too fast.

In the midst of it all, however, we discovered God's intervention again. The reason I was being hustled from one machine to the other was that the radiology department had a big conference going on after lunch. Had I not had the tests before lunch, there wouldn't have been anyone there to read the X rays. So I did my time on the CAT scan machine and, likewise, the bone scan machine. Then I returned to Dr. Monsen's waiting room to await the results.

Just before the lunch hour, I heard my name called again and I walked down the same hall to Dr. Monsen's office. As I entered, he was holding up another X ray. "Mr. Burkett, my suspicion was correct. You have a primary tumor in your right kidney. Because that is the primary tumor, and the one in your shoulder is secondary, I'm going to send you to another physician, Dr. Sam Graham. He's one of the best urological oncologists around. I've scheduled an appointment for you on Friday afternoon."

Dr. Monsen patiently took the next few minutes to help Judy and me understand what he was saying. He explained that both the kidney and shoulder cancers were operable and that there was some good news. The CAT scan detected no other tumors in my body. So while my condition was serious, and there were many unknown factors, Dr. Monsen also gave us some positive facts upon which to build our hope.

I think this is a lesson that any oncologist can benefit from. Emphasize the positive things to the patient, as well as telling the truth about the negative things. Everyone needs hope. So many times doctors unknowingly destroy that hope by plunging patients into despair, allowing them to think there is no hope. Maybe from a medical perspective it looks pretty bleak, but if the patient believes there is hope, I'll guarantee you that a positive mental attitude is going to work more toward the success of any therapy than a negative attitude.

And let me assure you, God's people can suffer from despair and depression—just like anybody else. We'd like to think that we have a perfect relationship with Christ that will overcome any obstacle but, in truth, we are still human beings. We live in frail bodies that are wearing out, and we have to come to grips with that. So even though Dr. Monsen had difficult news for me, he also gave me some positive medical news that helped to build hope.

That wasn't the case with a friend of mine who later was diagnosed with cancer. In his case, his doctor simply walked in and announced, "Listen, you have melanoma of the lung—a very fast-growing cancer that is often fatal. There's no hope for you and you'll probably die. You might have six months." And with that, the doctor simply walked out of the room and went to another patient.

Although I prefer for people to be direct with me, I guess that's an example of going beyond directness to the point of being callous. Fortunately, this kind of doctor is not the norm. But many times medical technicians get so caught up in their own busy schedules that they forget that they're dealing with living, breathing people.

I'm often asked, as a part of my daily radio program, "How is it that you can be so nice to people who call day after day, often with the same questions?" My response is, "I just remind myself each day that the questions asked by those particular listeners are the most important questions in their lives at the time." I believe medical technicians also need to remember that. Although they have seen the same disease a thousand times and experienced the same result the majority of the time, each patient deserves a personal response.

Remember Sgt. Joe Friday from the TV series, *Dragnet?* His famous line was, "The facts, Ma'am, just the facts." Well, if you're diagnosed with a terminal illness like cancer, you don't want somebody just to walk in and drop the facts on you and then leave. In my opinion, that's the height of callousness and demonstrates a lack of caring.

GOD IS IN CONTROL

It's interesting to note that, at times, I felt like a third-party observer of what was going on. Even as Dr. Monsen told me what he considered to be the bad news, I was looking at it objectively, as I would if I were a counselor looking into somebody else's life. When my fears and anxiety were aroused, my counsel to myself was the same I would give to anyone else: God is in control.

God knew all of this from the beginning of creation. He knew that I would be there that day in Dr. Monsen's office, that he would diagnose a malignancy in my left shoulder and my right kidney. The news did not take God by surprise. I had the distinct impression that God was telling me, "Don't worry."

The thing I continued to pray for, silently and verbally, after leaving Dr. Monsen's office, was that God would give me *peace* through this whole process. I truly believe God granted those prayers.

NO STRANGER TO EMERGENCY PHONE CALLS

As we returned home that afternoon from Dr. Monsen's office, we drove in silence. I suppose we were trying to comprehend it all. My thoughts replayed the urgent phone call I had received at the cabin in North Carolina only two days before. "You need to get back here right now," the radiologist had said. His tone had been urgent. Now I knew why.

Hospitals. Emergency phone calls. Life-threatening circumstances. It all had a familiar feel to it. The thoughts triggered an unsettling reminder of another emergency phone call I had received in 1985, when I was teaching a Christian Business Men's Committee Conference in Chattanooga, Tennessee.

That call came about 6:00 A.M., when I was startled from my sleep by a loud knocking on the door of my hotel room. When I opened the door, there stood Ted DeMoss, the president of the Christian Business Men's Committee.

"Larry, you've got a call downstairs from a hospital and they say it's urgent."

Needless to say, I quickly threw on some clothes and headed downstairs to answer the call. When I picked up the phone, the caller was an emergency room nurse from Northside Hospital in Atlanta, informing me that my son, Dan, had been involved in a very serious automobile accident. In fact, she said, "We're scheduling him for emergency surgery in a few minutes. I urge you to hurry." She went on to explain just how critical he was. He was unconscious. The paramedics had taken him to Northside Hospital because it was a trauma center, and the doctors would have to operate to save his life.

Of course, Judy and I threw our things into the car and raced back from Chattanooga, Tennessee to the hospital in Atlanta, stopping only long enough to call my pastor, Dr. Charles Stanley, to request prayer during the Sunday morning worship services. During the two-hour drive, two thoughts dominated my mind: Clearly, first I was concerned about my son's spiritual condition. Though he said he was a Christian, he wasn't living for the Lord, and I was sincerely concerned that perhaps he wasn't saved at all. So my first preoccupation was just asking God to spare him long enough to confirm his salvation.

Second, the accident couldn't have come at a worse time for me personally. Not that *any* time is good or appropriate for a loved one to have a wreck, but due to the schedule I had been keeping I was battling burnout. I just couldn't fathom how I could handle yet another crisis in my life.

To answer these concerns, God impressed several truths upon my heart during that drive to Atlanta. Foremost, there just isn't anything more important in life than eternal salvation, especially for your loved ones. It's not that I hadn't thought about this before, but I always thought I would have more time or that there would be a better opportunity later to talk about it.

Obviously God knew our hearts. We wanted our son to live, as any parents would. Certainly Judy and I prayed for that. It was the earnest prayer of our hearts. But in truth, I cared more about the salvation of my son than I did for his life here on earth. Life here is for a short time—just a breath—but eternity is forever.

When you don't know if one of your family members is going to live or die within the next hour, eternal issues come into clear focus. Frankly, it becomes an issue of whether you're going to see them again—ever. The simple truth is this: *God offers eternal salvation to all who place their trust in Jesus Christ as Savior and Lord.* An eternity of torment awaits those who reject His means of salvation. I loved Dan, and I wanted to *know* beyond a shadow of a doubt that he was saved. That's all I asked God for at the time.

We all live in temporal bodies that aren't going to last forever.

In fact, the apostle Paul says in 1 Corinthians 15:50, *"Now I say this, brethren, that flesh and blood cannot inherit the kingdom of God; nor does the perishable inherit the imperishable."* So whether I die from cancer, or heart disease, or an automobile accident—whatever—one day I'm going to exit life here on this earth, and you will too. There is no more important task in this life than to be ready to meet your Maker.

God addressed my second concern through another passage of Scripture: *"I can do all things through Him who strengthens me"* (Philippians 4:13). I took God at His word. I couldn't imagine how I could bear any more in my life at the time, but I trusted that God would sustain me.

When Judy and I arrived at Northside Hospital, we quickly made our way to the emergency area. Too late. Dan had already been wheeled away into the operating room. So we sat and waited.

During that initial three and one-half hour surgery, there were several times when a nurse emerged from behind the operating room doors. Our hopes were dashed with her message: "Prepare yourselves for the worst, because it looks like Dan is not going to make it." Once she brought news that Dan's kidneys were beginning to fail. Thirty minutes later, she returned to say that his lungs were failing. She tried to be sensitive, but there are not any pleasant ways to tell parents that their son is about to die.

Judy and I held each other, we prayed, and we awaited the outcome of the surgery.

While we were waiting for news about Dan, something happened inside of me. God answered my prayers with a spirit of peace. In fact, it was overwhelming. Like the apostle Paul, I have to say that it was *"the peace of God, which surpasses all comprehension"* (Philippians 4:7). Never before had I experienced such total peace about anything.

I had been praying for peace for months during the early phases of what I would call "burnout," when I was traveling and teaching all the time. We had all kinds of problems going on with the ministry staff at the time; we had just moved the ministry to a new location in north Georgia, and that move triggered a lot of stress. But in the midst of what had to be the biggest crisis of my life—waiting to hear whether my son Dan would live—God sent His peace and it just overwhelmed me. And I came to the realization that all the other things were really trivial compared to life or death, salvation or damnation.

I really wanted to share that peace with somebody, especially with Judy, but I couldn't at that time. I felt it was a very private thing between the Lord and me. Never, except during the initial period of my own salvation, had I ever truly experienced the awesome power and peace of our Lord. God just simply took me in His hands and relieved me of all my burdens. By experiencing His peace, I began to rest in the Lord and wait patiently for His reply.

For some reason, I had total confidence that God already had answered my prayers and that He would not allow Dan to die until I knew that he was saved and would be with God in heaven for eternity.

After what seemed like an eternity to us, a nurse emerged from the operating room with the message that we were to meet the surgeons in the family conference room. Dan had survived the operation. Thank God! Judy and I were elated and wept tears of joy.

The celebration did not last long, however. Within minutes, the surgeons entered the family conference room and began to outline a grim picture of Dan's condition. True, he had miraculously survived the operation to remove the bone chips from his sinus cavity, to set the obvious broken bones, and to suction out tiny pieces of shattered automobile that he had breathed into his lungs. The bad news, however, was that Dan had slipped into a very deep coma.

For nearly three months, Dan remained in that coma. During that time there was virtually no external indication that he was alive other than his heart rate, his respiration, and a little brain activity. Nonetheless, the doctors and nurses encouraged us to continue talking to him, even though he could not talk back to us. We did have some encouraging signs. Whenever I would speak to him, the monitors showed that his heart and respiration rates would increase; and, even though he didn't regain consciousness, I was confident that somewhere in Dan's subconscious he recognized my voice.

I am totally convinced that somewhere inside my son, perhaps all the way down in his spirit, he knew I was there and that gave him courage and confidence—much the same as God's Spirit deep within us gives us confidence to go on, no matter what the circumstances are.

During Dan's entire confinement, someone from our family remained at the hospital. We took turns reading Scripture to him or playing Christian music for him. And the medical staff at the hospital were just tremendous. Many of them were Christians and that enabled us to share a common bond, something that often is lacking in these situations. I always will be grateful for their dedication and hard work.

God delivered Dan from his coma after seventy-nine days. I can report to you that today he is doing very well. He has had a number of physical problems as a result of the car accident, including a hip reconstruction but, overall, he's managed to get on with his life. The one thing I now know for sure is that he is a Christian, and that was what I asked of God above all else.

BACK HOME: TIRED BUT NOT SLEEPY

As we pulled into our neighborhood back in Gainesville, I thought to myself, *Unbelievable!* In less than forty-eight hours, my schedule, indeed my world, had been turned upside down. Instead of completing the *Women Leaving the Workplace* manuscript, I was facing not one but two potential cancer surgeries: one to remove my right kidney and the next to remove my left shoulder blade. And for all I knew, the cancer could have spread to other places as yet unseen.

The next day, Thursday, promised two more huge hurdles to manage. To minimize rumors and misinformation, I decided to meet with the CFC staff, level with them about my situation, and seek their prayers. And later that same day, I planned to go on "Money Matters," our daily, live, call-in program, and talk about my diagnosis. No one could predict what impact my health status would have on the CFC ministry. We could only pray that support would remain steady and that God's people would respond positively. But we couldn't know for sure.

With my future looking so uncertain, sleep proved again to be an elusive commodity that night. There were doubts about the future, and I would have to be totally honest and say that I had some deep-seated fear. It wasn't so much the fear of dying; I'd pretty well come to grips with that. I knew that death was inevitable and the timing was up to God. Obviously! So it wasn't the dying so much as it was the fear of dying *with cancer.* At that time, I hadn't known many people with cancer, but I had known a few and their deaths had not been very pleasant. It had robbed them of their dignity. I didn't want that. But who does?

Wednesday had been a long, trying day. I was very tired but still too keyed up to be sleepy. My mind was racing too fast with thoughts. One of the things that really ministered to me that evening was our local Christian radio station. I turned to WRAF out of Toccoa Falls, Georgia and listened to Frank Nagle, their late-night personality. Frank just happened to be playing some music that night that really appealed to me. The theme of the songs centered around the kingdom of God, His glory, and how it's going to be for eternity with the Lord. I listened to a lot of great music from Keith Green, the Gaithers, Sandi Patty, and perhaps my favorite female vocalist, Cynthia Clawson. The music ministered to me and I was uplifted.

But Frank also shared specific Scriptures from God's Word that seemed to be just for me. I had read them before, but it's interesting when you hear them from somebody else at a time of crisis like this, the verses seem to have a different meaning. By the next morning, I felt that I was ready to go and face whatever difficulties I would have in getting rid of this cancer.

I was determined to fight. I knew that as long as God wanted me on this earth and He had a plan for my life, *nobody could take me.* And when God's plan for my life was finished and God no longer wanted me here, nothing could keep me here. Satan might think he could kill me, but I knew he couldn't.

As in the case of Job, God has built a hedge about His people and, to the extent that we're able to believe Him and trust Him, that hedge will stand firm. In God's plan for my life, the hedge was low enough to allow heart problems and cancer problems to afflict me, but somehow that evening I believed that God's hedge was not low enough to allow the angel of death to overcome me. I firmly took confidence in that as I faced the future.

I didn't get a lot of sleep the next few days, but I did get in a lot of praying. I was both focused and fervent in my prayers. Two passages of Scripture encouraged me as I prayed.

Jesus said in Matthew 7:11, *"If you then, being evil, know how to give good gifts to your children, how much more shall your Father who is in heaven give what is good to those who ask Him!"* I don't think we should be afraid to ask God for anything that, from our perspective, seems to be reasonable. So I prayed that this tumor would be harmless and benign, if it was God's will for me. As children of God, I believe we're free to come before Him with pure and innocent requests and tell Him exactly what's on our minds, as long as we remember it's *God's* decision. That's why I personally always temper my prayers with the caveat "if it is Your will."

In His most intense hour of trial, Jesus openly asked the Father to let the cup pass from Him; *"Yet not as I will, but as Thou wilt"* (Matthew 26:39). His example was to be completely honest with the Father about what was truly on His heart: *"Father, . . . let this cup pass."* Yet, in the same breath He submitted Himself to the sovereign will of God when he added *"as Thou wilt."*

The second passage of Scripture motivated the intensity of my prayers. *"The effective prayer of a righteous man can accomplish much"* (James 5:16). Since I believe that all who call on the name of the Lord are declared righteous by His blood, I knew this passage included me. The thrust of the verse means that "prayer changes things," and I certainly wanted the Lord to change my circumstances.

Most of all I asked the Lord for peace, His peace. I have experienced a lot of trauma in my life, and I know what it's like to live both with God's peace and without it—and I'll choose *with it* every time.

Here's what Jesus promised: *"Peace I leave with you; My peace I give to you; not as the world gives, do I give to you. Let not your heart be troubled, nor let it be fearful"* (John 14:27). I wanted God's peace in my life to counter the anxieties that cancer brings with it.

In John 16:33, Jesus said, *"These things I have spoken to you, that in Me you may have peace. In the world you have tribulation, but take courage; I have overcome the world."*

CHAPTER THREE

✦

Talking About It

For well over a decade, the radio studio at Christian Financial Concepts has broadcast the Good News of Jesus Christ, with particular attention being given to the biblical principles of managing money. I love talking with God's people and helping them with practical questions. It always has been both a challenge and a joy to serve our listeners in this way. And God has richly blessed our ministry. What began as a series of five-minute, taped programs, aired on a dozen stations, has mushroomed into an outreach that touches hundreds of thousands of people daily.

INSIDE THE STUDIO

I've entered the studio hundreds of times over the last ten years to do live programs and to tape others and, in great part, it has become fairly routine.

But when I entered the studio on that Thursday in 1995, to do the live "Money Matters" program, it was not a routine day. Less than twenty-four hours after learning that I had two tumors in my body, I stepped into the studio, closed the door, and prepared to tell our listeners that I likely had renal cell carcinoma—a deadly form of cancer.

The following is an excerpt of what the audience heard when Steve Moore, my co-host, opened the program at precisely 3:30 P.M. EST.

"Today on 'Money Matters,' a special message from our host, financial teacher and author, Larry Burkett. 'Money Matters' is produced by Christian Financial Concepts, a nonprofit ministry teaching biblical principles for handling money. If you need help with a financial question, call 1-800-525-7000. The Bible says it's God's will for us to be joyful always, to pray continually, and to give thanks in all circumstances. Sometimes that's difficult to do but, in the face of a trial, God is there to lead us and to love us. We'll talk with Larry about why that assurance is so important to him right now.

"Larry, God's Word says that we live in earthen vessels and our bodies are subject to decay and disease. Yesterday you received some medical news that reminds us all how frail our bodies really are. The doctors say that you have two tumors: one in your right kidney and the other in your left shoulder."

Larry: *"Yes. Big shock."*

Steve: *"Big shock to you, big shock to all of us. That news is difficult to take, but I do know, because you've talked to all of us as a staff, that you're trying to do as the Scripture says and to trust in the Lord."*

Larry: *"I try to do that, Steve, and I've tried to do that consistently since I've been a Christian. All of us fail sometimes, but I believe* the Lord is still in control of all things, including my body. I don't know why this has happened. I had a sore shoulder—you and I both know we talked about it a lot of times."

Steve: "Yes, for months."

Larry: "Yeah, and I just kept looking for an answer, and I thought it would be an orthopedic answer. Finally about a week ago the doctor said, 'I don't know. I finally give up. Go get an MRI,' which is a machine that looks inside your body. I had actually gone up to our cabin in North Carolina to do some writing, trying to catch up on a book I'm writing, and got a call from my doctor, and he said, 'Time to come home! Bad news! You've got a tumor in your shoulder.' That was a shock—a real shock! It takes a while to adjust to that. Then he sent me over to Emory University. . .Crawford Long Hospital, actually."

Steve: "In Atlanta?"

Larry: "Yes, I went there yesterday. I went through a bone scan and a CAT scan and they found I had a tumor on my right kidney that has apparently been there for a period of time, and it also now has appeared in my left shoulder. You know, in all things we're to give thanks, Steve, and I can't say that I've adjusted to this yet. My emotions are still up and down, you know, sometimes they're real high and sometimes they're real low."

Steve: "Well, it's been less than twenty-four hours."

Larry: "Well, that's pretty normal. But I can sure see God's hand. Had I not hurt my shoulder playing golf, I never would have started looking for an answer. I had no reason to believe I had a problem. I'd passed physicals every year—I just passed a physical the latter part of last year but, because my shoulder kept hurting, I kept looking for an answer. Most probably they'll have to take the kidney out. That'll be the normal routine. I've got to go back again tomorrow for kind of a final diagnosis with a renal specialist, but I would assume that's what they're going to do. What we'll do with the shoulder, we don't know. Probably they'll have to decide before the first operation.

"We do live in earthen vessels. I've said that before many, many times. I've faced death once before in my life and I wasn't afraid. I don't think I'm afraid now. I don't feel afraid. I don't like the process. Hospitals aren't my favorite things and knives aren't my favorite tools, but God's will be done."

Steve: *"Larry, the ministry of Christian Financial Concepts—the future of CFC—what do you see long term?"*

Larry: *"Well, I trust that it will go on, with or without me. I'd like to stay around a little bit longer to help guide it down the path. But if this ministry is dependent on me, if it's really dependent on me, it is not from God. But, I believe this ministry will succeed and survive, irrespective of whether or not Larry Burkett is here."*

Steve: *"Larry, you've been through some tough times in the past. You've had some heart problems, you've had some eye problems, your son Danny almost died a few years ago, and through it all you came back much stronger and with a much greater faith in God than ever before."*

Larry: *"I believe that one of the primary purposes of God putting us through this, Steve, is to bring us closer to Him, and we keep saying that. As I've said many times, it's easy to say you trust God; it's another thing to trust God. I pray others will pray with me just for that purpose."*

Steve: *"I'm sure they will. We'll be right back after this"* (cut to station break).

TALKING ABOUT IT WASN'T EASY

I'm told that there wasn't a dry eye in our offices that afternoon. No one likes to be the bearer of bad news, especially when you know what you say will bring sadness to others. It was not easy for me to tell my family and friends that I had cancer. Neither was it easy to go on the air and relay the news to the nation.

The counsel I had from some friends was to not tell anybody about my health condition and, particularly, not over the air.

Their concern was that our listeners, who are in great part our supporters of the ministry, would believe that I was terminally ill and that the ministry would no longer be worthy of their support. I took that into consideration and I appreciated their honesty, but I also believe God honors total honesty. And even more than that—far beyond the monetary sense—the thing I wanted most was the prayers of God's people.

James 5:16 says *"The effective prayer of a righteous man can accomplish much."* I believe the earnest prayers of many righteous men and women avail even more.

If I honestly thought that God's people would not support the ministry of Christian Financial Concepts simply because I was sick or if, in fact, I died, I would shut down the ministry, because that would mean it was built on a person and not on the Lord. Praise God that's not true. And praise God that His people, being the most marvelous people in the world, responded positively to my news.

If you have an initial resistance to talking about troubling medical news, or any other major problem, you're not alone. I know what that feels like. But let me encourage you that the healthiest thing to do is to talk out the situation you're facing with those who are closest to you. There are a number of reasons why.

1. Telling others about your predicament helps you to peel back layers of denial.

Things happened so quickly for me that I had a difficult time adjusting. I needed time to think it all through and sort out the implications of my health. As I said earlier, there were times when I felt like an outside, impartial observer, as though the bad news was someone else's problem. That's all a natural function of denial. It's too easy to think there's a mistake with the tests, that it's all a bad dream, or to rationalize it all away.

Talking about it with Judy, my family, and our staff at the ministry had a powerful, beneficial impact on me: *It helped me to face reality.* That's because there's something very powerful about the element of vocalization. You can have a thousand different thoughts and intentions floating around in your head, but they never seem to become reality unless you *vocalize* the thoughts.

Obviously you can overdo discussion, and some people dwell so much on their problems that's all they ever want to talk about. But normally that's not during the early stages of a health crisis. That constant barrage of negative talk usually comes after the crisis is over, and they keep going over it again and again. It's little more than a form of self-pity. I think it's one thing to talk about your problems and to be honest with people, but it's quite another thing to make that the center of all your conversation for the rest of your life. It is not God's will for us to dwell continually on the past, and it's certainly not God's will for us as a people to feel sorry for ourselves.

As I've shared with many of my friends since this happened to me, "Don't feel sorry for me. I have faced death and I've come to grips with it. I think I understand it, and I accept its inevitability, whether it happens right now or twenty years from now. Instead, feel sorry for those people who haven't faced it, because now or in fifty years they will have to confront their fears."

I think God created us with a built-in overload switch. In times of shock, like bad news about cancer or the death of a loved one, God has built within us a mechanism to shut down our minds temporarily. It's almost like a circuit breaker that trips to keep us from absorbing too much during that time. But time is a great healer, and after a little time passes our ability to function and think should return. If it doesn't, again we must consider that a spiritual imperfection needs to be dealt with.

But the problems can multiply exponentially if we ignore reality. For instance, it's not unusual for people to ignore symptoms of poor health—blood in the urine, rectal bleeding, high blood pressure, to name a few—hoping that the problems will go away. And rather than talk to their doctors or even their families about the symptoms, a mental wall of denial is constructed, leaving a smoldering fire to erupt into a huge, perhaps life-threatening, inferno.

The very act of vocalization forces us to put into words what we're feeling. Talking to others helped me to face the serious condition I had. In fact, as Judy pointed out, once I had discussed it with others and told them what I had, there was no way I could back out of going to the hospital, which was her greatest concern. She knows how I feel about hospitals, and she worried that somehow I would decide, "Nope. Not for me. I can tough this out like I've toughed out so many other things."

So it was a great comfort to her to know that I'd told many people the diagnosis and the prospective treatment, as well as my commitment to show up at Dr. Graham's office that upcoming Friday. Ultimately I would undergo the procedures to remove my right kidney and, most likely, my left shoulder blade.

2. If you talk about your health, your family and friends also will feel free to talk about it.

Most often those around you will mirror your attitude and response to your health situation. If you clam up, deny it, or act like nothing is wrong, it's likely others will too. However, if you openly discuss what's on your heart, you'll trigger candid, heartfelt responses from your loved ones.

I can remember a good friend several years ago who'd adopted a philosophy that he thought was totally biblical. He never spoke negative words or thoughts around other people, and he did not allow other people to speak anything negative around him. Well, I'm sure there are some positives associated with cancer but, at the time, I couldn't think of very many. Perhaps now, looking back, I can find some positives, but at the time they were hard to come by.

Unfortunately, if, as in my friend's case, you have made it a biblical mandate to never speak negatives and never accept negatives from anybody else, very possibly you'll go into denial. Then others will tell you everything is great, and you'll agree everything is great, and it won't change the circumstances—at all. If you believe your positive mental attitude will entice God to supernaturally heal you, your "faith" is in for a rude awakening. Understand, that doesn't mean to adopt a negative attitude.

When Dan was in the coma, I asked the doctors and nurses not to speak negatives in his presence. But that was because they were near enough for him to hear, even though he was in a coma. I was concerned that deep in his mind, which was still active, he could hear them talking. But that's totally different from saying to somebody, "I don't want to talk about cancer. I don't have cancer. I choose to deny it."

I rather suspect that a great many people who have done that in the past have died of their illness when, in fact, God had a cure that would have worked for them—only it wasn't a "miraculous" cure.

I think of a story I heard a long time ago about a man who was trapped on his roof during a flood. He was clinging to the chimney, praying that God would supernaturally rescue him. A fellow came by in a boat and asked if he could help, but the man said, "No, no. Don't worry about it. It's under control. God's going to rescue me." So the man in the boat went on.

The water continued to rise and another fellow came by paddling a skimpy little raft and said, "You know, the water is getting pretty deep. Can I help you?" Still clinging to his chimney, the man replied, "No, no. Don't worry about it. God's going to rescue me." And the man in the raft also went on downstream.

The water rose higher and higher, all the way up to his knees. About then, a helicopter flew over, and the pilot shouted down, "I'll lower a rope." But the man replied, "No, no. God has this under control. He's going to rescue me." So the helicopter went on. The water continued to rise, covering the house, sweeping the man away to his death.

When the man showed up in heaven, St. Peter met him at the gates. The man was deeply disillusioned and said, "Peter, I believe God failed me." When Peter asked why he believed such a thing, the man replied, "Well, God promised that He was going to rescue me, and yet He didn't. I drowned instead."

Peter smiled as he replied, "Well, my friend, He sent three different people by to pick you up and you turned them all away. What did you expect?"

Of course, that's a fictitious story, but the principle cannot be lost. Often God uses natural things to rescue His people. They are not always those instantaneous, miraculous answers that we see sprinkled through God's Word.

Open the Conversation Yourself. It may be awkward to discuss your situation at first, especially if your family is not in the habit of talking openly together. You may have to swallow some pride, but awkward conversations can quickly be eased by true, heartfelt sharing. I think sometimes people hold back from talking about the prospect of dying, believing that if they talk about dying it might make it happen; or if they don't talk about it, that might prevent it from happening.

But let me assure you, that's not the case. Openly discussing the prospect of death (without dwelling on it) will not accelerate it. Remember, as long as God wants us on this earth, nothing can remove us; and when God no longer wants us on this earth, nothing can retain us.

Think of it like this. If you are sick, that's true whether you talk about it or not. So why not acknowledge the issue and begin to deal with it? Probably, if you're reading this book, either you or a loved one is facing some stressful, threatening issues, and that's a lot to cope with. But *don't do it alone.* Everyone should have someone who understands what's going on inside them emotionally, mentally, and spiritually—including you.

There are many people around the country, perhaps even thousands, that I consider friends; and I trust they consider me a friend. But there really aren't that many people I consider to be *close* friends: those who know me so well they know how I feel and they accept me with all my weaknesses and with all my "warts," so to speak. Those friends are really precious to me.

During the time I was undergoing this crisis, I was able to share with several of them exactly what I was feeling, without any fear that somehow they might think less of me as a human being. Once again, let me say that I had a lot of doubts and many fears during this time. It wasn't death I feared. It was the process of dying. It was a peculiar feeling to actually envy those who had already died. As the modern saying goes: Been there, done that!

One piece of advice I would give anyone: Open up, share with your family, and let them help. Make them insiders to what is going on. Don't make them outsiders. They'll feel a lot more comfortable, they'll understand better, and they'll be there to help.

3. Talking can help to clarify your thoughts.

When I think back, the course of events unfolded at lightning speed. On one Monday, March 13, I arose to type on a book manuscript. On Wednesday, March 15, I learned that I not only had a tumor in my left shoulder, I had a tumor in my right kidney. And by Friday, March 17, I found myself in a second doctor's office discussing the removal of my right kidney through a procedure called a radical nephrectomy.

Days later, I was checking into Emory University to undergo major surgery for the removal of my right kidney. The days in between were an absolute blur. It was hard to find time alone just to sit down, think, grasp the significance of what I was facing, and begin to cope.

In the absence of much private time, however, I found it helped to talk. There were so many things to think about, my mind seemed to be on overload. My thoughts were a flat line, except for the subject of cancer but, constantly, my thoughts were scurrying ahead to the dreaded prospect of an operation. I think I probably dreaded the operations more than I did the prospect of cancer.

I never have particularly liked hospitals, though I appreciate what they do, but the smell and the austere look dredge up some bad memories. I often wonder why they don't paint hospitals pretty colors and put up some wallpaper and make it look more like a motel or hotel than a hospital. It was fortunate for me that we were able to arrange these events so quickly I didn't have time to ponder them. Very likely, Judy would have been correct: I might have talked myself out of the planned operations if I'd had long enough to think about it.

Yet, talking to Judy and my family helped to work it out. I'm so thankful to God for my family and friends. We helped each other to more or less establish an "equilibrium" about what was going on. When one of us got down, the others could comfort, console, encourage, and pray. We helped one another to be strong. The ability to talk openly was the key that allowed us to minister to one another.

Think back to the time when you were in school. Did you ever have a math problem you couldn't solve, yet, you knew you had the answer somewhere inside? Try as you might, it was just impossible to come up with the right solution on your own—that is, until you talked about it with someone else (I'm talking about homework, *not a test*). In the very process of discussing it you found that you had the answer all along. I believe that's not only true with math word problems, it's also true with life's problems. When you discuss or tell others of your situation, you actually help to work out a solution.

What seems so incredibly confusing at the moment can begin to clear up if you will share openly with others. But *you must let them know,* and that leads to my next point.

4. When you talk about your real needs, others discover how to help you.

I've seen people sit around and sulk, or pout, because they have needs that are being overlooked. Even though they are desperately lonely or afraid, their pride confines them to silence, thus cutting off the very help they need. Often over time they become bitter and resentful because their needs are not being met. If that sounds childish, it is. That's just the way little children act.

The apostle Paul wrote *"When I was a child, I used to speak as a child, think as a child, reason as a child; when I became a man, I did away with childish things"* (1 Corinthians 13:11).

Pretending that nothing is wrong will not make your circumstances change. If you know what your needs are, then say so. Even if you don't know what your needs are, voice the fact that you are hurting. That's why God put other people in the world: to be able to help you when you aren't functioning at 100 percent.

5. Talking encourages honesty with yourself, with your family, and with God.

As I mentioned earlier, several years ago I went through what might be called a mid-life crisis, or burnout, or stress overload; I was just having a tough time coping. I was doing a lot of seminars all over the country, ministering to other people, and I became mentally fatigued. At the same time, I was having some difficulty with our staff and my mind just wasn't coping very well.

Following my son's automobile accident, when I had lots of time to reflect, I took an honest look at myself and decided to resign as manager of the universe. Somehow, prior to that time, I thought God's work wouldn't get done unless I did it; and God's people wouldn't hear about money unless I told them. To a large degree, I felt like the unsaved wouldn't hear about Christ unless I told them. So everywhere I went, I shared with everybody—the person seated next to me on the airplane, people in elevators, cab-drivers—everybody. Obviously there is nothing wrong with sharing your faith, but I felt *compelled* to do it.

When people would write and ask me to come do a seminar, I felt I had to go because the Lord had provided the opportunity. Or if they asked me to speak at a conference, I felt that I *had* to go. I realize now that I was driving myself toward collapse.

I can remember sitting in that hospital room with Dan and honestly talking it out with the Lord. I confessed to Him that I had taken on responsibilities that He had never given to me. The truth is, God's work is going to get done whether Larry Burkett does it or not, and God's people are going to hear His Word, whether I tell them or not. So that day in the hospital, I simply resigned as manager of the universe: a position that God had never appointed me to in the first place.

That decision relieved a great deal of stress for me. I also concluded that, although I knew I wasn't perfect, I wanted other people to know that I wasn't perfect as well. I felt that it would help my relationship with those I taught if they realized up front that I had flaws. I do. From that day forward, I have tried, to the best of my ability, to be totally honest with everybody. It's not that I tried to lie to them before, but I wasn't totally honest and visible. My goal from that day forward has been that others would say of me, "What you see is what you get," rather than "What you hear is different from who he is."

Talking with others about your situation breeds honesty, and I would encourage you to be honest about your thoughts and feelings. That doesn't mean to be pouty, whiny, and complaining. But if you're fearful of dying, tell someone around you. If you're not absolutely, positively sure about your salvation in Christ Jesus, then admit it. Call your pastor. If you don't have one, call a nearby Bible-teaching church and ask for a session with the pastor. If he's a man of God, he can help you settle the salvation issue— once and for all.

The one certainty I had was knowing that I was a Christian. I knew Christ was my Savior, and I knew absolutely where I was going to spend eternity, and that made facing the trials so much easier.

◆

CHAPTER FOUR

What Will Happen to the Ministry If . . . ?

So what does happen to a major Christian ministry when the leader becomes gravely ill . . . or dies? That was on my mind, as well as the minds of many of our supporters.

With the increased interest in Christian radio and television programs over the last two decades, there has been an increase of parachurch ministries that have flourished under the leadership of dynamic, charismatic-type people.

By parachurch ministries, I mean organizations that exist to complement and strengthen the local churches. Often these are large, sophisticated ministry organizations, developed to carry out the mission of the leaders: the Billy Graham Association, Focus on the Family, and Prison Fellowship are wonderful examples of such organizations. Christian Financial Concepts has a great support staff who work with me as well.

I suspect most of these leaders would reflect on the growth of their ministries the same way I do. The ministry of Christian Financial Concepts is not my invention or my creation. Instead, this ministry exists because of a calling from God. In His sovereign wisdom, God has chosen to work through those involved to fulfill His plan, and our involvement has been that of simple obedience—the same way Christian men and women all over America obey God in their lines of work.

Of course, when the leader of such an organization becomes ill, disabled, or even if the Lord calls him or her home, supporters often back off and wonder, "What will become of that ministry now?" That's a fair question, and a ministry's supporters deserve a direct answer.

I know the news of my cancer surgeries deeply concerned many people, including our own staff. In the back of our employees' minds was the concern for the future of Christian Financial Concepts and their jobs.

Often over the years I felt like I was simply hanging on to a moving vehicle being steered by the Lord in whatever direction He desired. Just as a spark plug can't take credit for the completion of a long trip, each one of us is an integral part of a complex mechanism that is being used and directed by the Lord to accomplish His purposes.

As is the norm in our society, people give praise and accolades to teachers and writers, but I have tried over the years not to let that go to my head because, in large part, we're stand-ins for what the Lord wants to accomplish. I truly believe that there is no greater reward in heaven for teaching, writing a book, or doing a radio program than there is for the person who answers the phone or cleans the building or for the ones who volunteer at the church nursery on Sundays to watch over God's most precious gift: children.

But it is a fact that people often associate a ministry with a particular individual, and certainly that's true of the founder who happens to be a teacher. So the doubt was in my mind during this period of time: *What will happen to the ministry if I die?*

The first question that must be asked is, is there a *need* for this ministry? One certainty I have about the ministry of Christian Financial Concepts is, there *is* need for such an organization. Clearly God calls us to be good stewards of the money He provides and, for the most part, as Americans, we have not been good stewards. That includes God's people.

The divorce rate among young couples is about 50 percent, and in the majority of these cases the finger can be pointed directly at their lack of financial wisdom as the source of their stress, their arguments, and ultimately the dissolution of their marriages.

Until we resolve this problem, there always will be a need for a ministry that teaches God's principles of handling money. That does not necessarily mean that it has to be CFC. But it would be a shame to make the investment that has been made in people, in training, even in buildings and equipment, and then not to be able to utilize them. So I believe that God has a purpose for this ministry and that He wants it to succeed.

How much would CFC be affected by the death of the founder? That's very difficult to say. We probably won't know until I die as, ultimately, I must. I trust, by that time, the ministry's transition away from a personality will have been made and God's people will accept this ministry for what it is: a tool created by God for God's purpose.

THE BOTTOM LINE

My heart's desire is to stick around a while longer and continue to serve the Lord here on earth. But, as I said before, if the ministry is built solely on me, and if it cannot survive without me, then it's not the work of God. To the contrary, we've seen God lead and supply the needs of this ministry in miraculous ways over the years. It's evident to me that He has not only called CFC into being, but it is by His will that we are sustained.

The key to the longevity of any organization is the training of people to carry on the work. If you review the ministry of Jesus, that's exactly what He did. In three years or less, He successfully discipled a group of men who carried on the work of the Gospel *in His absence.* Were His efforts successful? In hindsight, we can say "Yes" some 2,000 years later. His church is spread around the globe with over a billion people proclaiming the name of Jesus. My point is, His plan all along was to train leaders who could function in His absence.

So you can see why I'm neither alarmed nor overwhelmed at the thought of CFC's future, with or without me. From my perspective, He called this ministry into being; He has been faithful to us in the past; and He will continue to be our foundation in the future.

I have consistently told our staff: "This is God's ministry and He will supply our needs. The day He stops supplying our needs is the day we will close our doors, because there will no longer be a need for what we do. And I sincerely hope and pray there will be such a day. But until that day comes, our resolve is to continue advancing forward with the message of Christ."

CFC'S RICH HISTORY OF FAITH

Judy and I started Christian Financial Concepts out of the basement of our home in Tucker, Georgia (a suburb of Atlanta) in 1976 and, from the beginning, our vision was to see the body of Christ become good managers of their material resources. My heart was burdened by the number of Christians bringing grief and turmoil on themselves because they didn't follow God's principles in their handling of money.

Rather than "do" the work of ministry, my plan was to "train the church" to do that work of service. While that sounds simple, there's a world of difference between "doing" and "training others to do" this work. The first model leads to competition with the church; the second model leads to supplementing and complementing the church. The latter is the role I've always seen our ministry called to fulfill. Again, I believe this is the pattern that Jesus set.

In order for us to help train the church to live by biblical principles of handling money, it was necessary to identify and train counselors within the local churches who could do the face-to-face counseling with people in need. Second, we needed training materials to work with. This need eventually led to the writing and publication of my first workbook, *How to Manage Your Money* in 1975, and *The Financial Planning Workbook* in 1979.

To really get in the groove of training counselors across the United States, I felt like God was leading us to establish a national training center in 1983. After much prayer and searching, we set our sights on the purchase of a 200-acre tract of land, complete with a lake and numerous existing buildings, tucked away in the beautiful hills of north Georgia, outside of the old gold-mining town of Dahlonega.

The year we signed the agreement to buy the property, our total annual operating budget was $125,000 and the total property costs were $325,000, or almost three times our annual budget. Without advertising, promoting, or begging people for funds, we began praying for God to deliver the total amount, because we were committed to not borrowing.

The closing on the property was set for 2:00 P.M. on Friday at the Bank of Dahlonega. A good attorney friend of the ministry, Bob Field, handled the closing for us, and we drove up to Dahlonega together after lunch. On the way, Bob asked, "How are we doing for funds?"

I said, "Well, pretty good. We raised $225,000."

His comment was, "Well, I hope you know we need $325,000 to close." I did, and if we failed to close, we would forfeit $20,000 in option money that one of our board members had put up for us. To be sure, I was a little concerned, and I think you would be too, driving to a closing, knowing that we were $100,000 short of the needed amount.

Unknown to us, while I was on the way to Dahlonega, a friend called the office to see how the fund raising was going. My secretary told him, "Larry said we're doing okay, and that we've raised $225,000."

"How much do you need?" the man asked.

"We need $325,000 to close," she replied.

I know you're ahead of me now. Yes, during the drive to Dahlonega, the man wired the additional $100,000 to the bank. Praise God! Were we surprised and relieved when we got to the bank! I realize that circumstances don't always mean that it's God's will, but since we believed that God was calling us to this work, and the funds were provided in a miraculous, timely fashion, we accepted that we were following God's will for the ministry.

OVERCOMING EARLY MEDIA BIAS

Moving the CFC ministry offices from Atlanta to Dahlonega was not without some grief. To understand, you really have to know a little about north Georgia culture. Since the Blue Ridge mountains spill over into this area, the terrain is marked by gorgeous foothills, blanketed by hardwoods and pine trees, rushing trout streams, and breathtaking waterfalls. Private lakes, tucked away between the mountains, are a fishing paradise. To be sure, there's something beautiful and invigorating about sitting in a canoe, watching the sun rise over the mountains, and seeing their towering reflection on the perfectly calm, mirror-like surface of a lake. The property we purchased had just such a ten-acre lake. In fact, the property was known in the community as Hidden Lake.

The planned move to Dahlonega was not without some trepidation for me personally. I'm very much a people person, and I love to be around people. If I'm isolated from people for more than just a few days, I get really antsy. Knowing that, I was reluctant to move to such a small community: Dahlonega is a small town of about 2,500, and the Hidden Lake property was located eight miles out of town. Compared to Atlanta, it was really out in the boonies.

As is typical of a small town where everybody knows everybody else's business, when the paperwork on the sale of the property went through the courthouse in Lumpkin County (of which Dahlonega is the county seat), one of the secretaries spotted the fact that a religious organization had purchased the Hidden Lake property.

Not knowing who we were, she became suspicious for this reason. When we bought the property, we actually made a tax-free exchange for the owner with a fellow by the name of Ray Mooney. When the secretary read this on the paper work, she must have said to herself, "A-ha! A religious organization and Mooney—the *Moonies!*" So she promptly called a major Atlanta television station and said, "Did you know the 'Moonies' are moving into north Georgia?"

So the station sent out a crew to cover this story. Now get the picture. Here it was, the middle of July in the South—a hot, sweltering time of year. Our first objective was to repair all the buildings on the property, beginning with putting a new roof on each.

Our construction crew was comprised of our contractor and a group of locals he had hired. Up on the roofs, the mountain men ripped off shingles in the blistering hot sun. All of them were stripped down to their blue jeans or bib-overalls, and many of them sported decade-old beards drenched in sweat and, yes, several were spitting tobacco over the roof's edge (hard hats were required for anyone working on the ground). And the flies, gnats, and mosquitoes? It was awful.

Into this scene drove the television news team. They spent about three hours interviewing people, including me. Of course, all the interviews were edited down to about three minutes. And what did they choose to air?

They had interviewed the local postal delivery woman. When they had asked her, "What do you think about the religious fanatics moving into north Georgia?" she replied, "Well, we don't want any religious fanatics up here, but we have found that these are fine Christian people, and we appreciate them being here."

As you might guess, to play up their story line, the station did not air the second part of her comment—just the first. So if you had listened to the evening news in Atlanta that night, what you would have heard is the reporter asking the postal delivery woman, "What do you think about the religious fanatics moving up here?" And her reply: "Well, we don't want any religious fanatics up here."

And of course, the video showed our construction crews right in the middle of a remodeling mess, long hair and beards, stripped to their waists, and spitting tobacco. Obviously, the negative publicity did not help our efforts to hire staff in this little north Georgia community. In fact, I had wondered if there were any Christians living in Dahlonega, because we were having so much difficulty hiring a secretary.

When we finally hired a local lady as a secretary, she confided to me just how cautious she was about working for us. She said, "When I told someone that I was going to work for your ministry, I was warned that, before long, I would be asked to turn over all my property and money to CFC, and that I would have to raise my kids in your school!"

And we didn't even have a school.

GROWTH BROUGHT NEW PROBLEMS

Needless to say, we had some early public relations problems to overcome in north Georgia. But here again, we found God's intervention on our behalf, and the ministry began to prosper. Prosperity sometimes is a mixed blessing, because with the growth of the ministry came additional problems for me.

While I was traveling all over the country, we were trying to rebuild the property at Hidden Lake. There were also significant problems with some of the staff who had moved up from Atlanta. They didn't really want to be there but felt like they would be denying the Lord's will if they didn't come along.

So each time I came back from a trip, I was faced with the pressures of additional problems found on the property: a staff who didn't like country living and a growing ministry that demanded more of my time. This was truly a mixed blessing but one that clearly was taking a toll on my health. Prior to that time, I don't think I had ever been sick more than a day in my life but, under the pressure, I progressively began to have more and more physical problems.

During the winters, I began to catch colds regularly. It seemed like I caught every flu that came by. Even during the summer I found myself being eaten by every insect in north Georgia, especially little critters we call "no-see-ums." A "no-see-um," I decided, is a dehydrated piranha that flies, and when they land on you, although you can't see them, they take huge bites out of your skin—at least they did mine.

In addition to these problems, I found I was about to face the greatest financial crisis that any ministry can face—a confrontation with the Internal Revenue Service.

GOD'S STRENGTH TO OVERCOME THE IRS

Shortly after we arrived in Dahlonega, I received a letter in the mail from the Internal Revenue Service saying that our ministry had been selected for an audit. I'd have to be honest and say that I wasn't looking forward to it, because I knew how time-consuming it would be. But neither was I worried about it. I knew that we had never done anything wrong. Since we paid our taxes in a timely and godly fashion, we really didn't have anything to fear. The one lesson I learned from the audit was that, although you don't have to fear the IRS, you had better respect it, because it can make your life quite miserable in the process of doing its job.

It was our misfortune to draw an agent who was brand new to the nonprofit auditing department, and he was eager to prove his competence. And although he didn't say so, he clearly let it be known that he suspected we were a bunch of crooks who were using a nonprofit organization for our own personal benefit.

With that mind-set, he began an audit that dragged on for the better part of fourteen months. During that time, he made my life as miserable as one human being can make another—legally, of course.

At the time, I was very naive about the process of an IRS audit. I made the comment, "Well, we don't have anything to hide. Let's just open up all our books," which is the *wrong way* to deal with the IRS. Instead, I learned the hard way that you need to make the IRS tell you what it wants, supply that specific information, and *don't* let it go fishing around in your files.

Well, "Sherlock Holmes" proceeded to go through the minutes to our staff meetings—not our board of directors minutes but the staff meetings, where we talked about a variety of issues, including building additional buildings, maybe selling off some property to people who would build homes and then let us use them—and all kinds of ideas. We never pursued most of them because they were either inappropriate or not within the confines of a nonprofit organization.

Anyway, the IRS agent presumed all those intentions were real, and no amount of arguing could convince him otherwise. I remember him saying to me, "I *know* that you've done something illegal, and I'm going to find it."

To give you an idea just how this audit went, the agent called me the day before the Thanksgiving holiday with this message: "Mr. Burkett, I've reviewed your files, and I believe you're guilty of misuse of your tax-exempt status. As of today, I'm recommending that the IRS freeze all the assets of your organization, Christian Financial Concepts." And then he hung up.

That really shook me up. I knew that we hadn't done anything wrong and that he didn't have any evidence to back up his claims. But there we were, at his mercy. And since it was right at Thanksgiving, I couldn't contact our attorney or our accountant for that entire weekend—Thursday through Sunday. And I had to sweat it out under the assumption that all of our assets had been frozen and checks would begin to bounce. And, of course, I grieved over how this would look in the newspapers: "Christian Organization That Teaches on Money Impounded by the IRS."

The stress was taking its toll. I found myself sleeping less and less. I had been able to get away with very little sleep in college, but now I was 45 years old.

I finally reached our attorney the first thing Monday morning and explained the latest hassle. He got right on the problem and called me back *with unbelievable news*—the agent had made a *mistake.* He told my attorney that *he really meant to call another organization instead.*

Hard to believe, but I was deeply thankful for God's intervention on our behalf; but it was also one more stress crack.

GOD IS GREATER

So you see, the news of my cancer was just one chapter in the ongoing story of CFC's history and development. Each step of the way has had its share of obstacles, which could only be overcome by faith in God's strong hand. Every opportunity provided a fresh, new way for God to demonstrate His power in and through us.

When Jesus promised in John 16:33 that we would have tribulation in this world, He understood from whence He spoke. Satan can and does rear his ugly head everywhere the Gospel is being proclaimed. The good news that we experienced is that Jesus Himself has overcome the world. We leaned on the truth of a key Bible verse in our attempts to cope with so many obstacles to our work. *"Greater is He who is in you than he who is in the world"* (1 John 4:4).

But from a human perspective, each event that we allow to put stress on us creates a potential health hazard in our lives. Looking back on it, I can clearly see how ridiculous it was to allow this stress to accumulate: the stress from too much travel because I couldn't say no to people; the stress from troublesome staff because I didn't say to them, "Go back home"; the stress from the IRS agent, even though I knew we were totally legal and hadn't done anything wrong.

Those are the weapons that Satan can use against us. He understands very clearly what our breaking points are, and, praise God, so does the Lord. But unfortunately, quite often we don't—or at least I didn't understand that at the time, and I just continued to load stress upon stress.

My encounter with the IRS was a significant point in my relationship with the Lord. God meant it for my greater good, and He knew that during the period more than ten years later, when I would be undergoing the cancer crisis, I would be able to look back at this period and remember *this too will pass*. God's love and strength are always greater than what we experience. That makes the passage from 1 John 4:4 all the more relevant. God, who dwells in us, really is *"greater than he who is in this world,"* and we need to focus on that at all times.

I can attest to the fact that the CFC organization is no stranger to overcoming obstacles. There were times when we felt like we were facing a sheer stone wall. We've had to rely on God's intervention and guidance each step of the way and, in retrospect, I can see His faithfulness each step of the way. Knowing that He has been faithful in the past helps us to have confidence as we face future trials and tribulations.

A WORD OF TESTIMONY

The following letter provides a glimpse into the way God continues to be at work through the CFC ministry. Words of encouragement like this confirm in my heart that the ministry will continue to be a source of blessing to God's people, even if I'm absent.

> "Dear Larry and CFC Staff,
>
> The enclosed gift represents just a small portion of our gratitude to you. This month we are celebrating paying off our $7,000 mortgage on our new home. We have no car or consumer debt whatsoever and we hope to be totally debt free within the next year (we have a student loan and medical bills).
>
> "Since becoming believers a few years ago, my husband and I have been discipled by CFC programs and materials.

Our family of four lives on my husband's $30,000 a year (before taxes) income from his own business. We live on less than $2,000 a month, yet I am amazed, like Elijah's widow, how the Lord stretches and provides because we truly live the abundant life and lack for nothing!

"Last year, when we were still about $70,000 in debt, we sold our beautiful 2,000 square foot home and built a cute 1,250 square foot cottage—almost unheard of around our area and among our friends! We are 'rebels' among our friends and family for our commitment to 'downward mobility.' Yet we are the happiest and most content we've ever been. Our finances have impacted our marriage, health, and spiritual growth!

"With our small house and simple life, I am not in bondage to housework, shopping, and materialism. My husband is free to serve more at our church, where he (with CFC's help) established and heads up a benevolence outreach ministry. Because of our financial freedom, he is also able to go on short-term mission and disaster relief trips.

"Please use this money wherever it is most needed. We have been wanting to contribute toward your new single's ministry but trust that you'll put it toward your most urgent needs or wants. We hope you'll keep growing and expanding so other lives can experience the freedom and blessings we have.

"Special thanks, also, to Mr. Chuck Thompson [the editor of CFC's monthly newsletter called *Money Matters*]. Once he spoke with me on the phone and just radiated Christ right through the phone lines! He was very helpful and gracious. We enjoy and pass along our newsletter every month.

"Only heaven will reveal the impact you all have had on our lives and so many others. Thanks for being faithful servants of our Lord."

Letters like that confirm that God is actively working through the CFC ministry. And again, it's all because of His grace and calling. It's not because of me or any other single person. It's God's calling upon our lives collectively.

CHAPTER FIVE

Surgery

*T*he days surrounding my two surgeries are somewhat of a blur. If you've ever had surgery, you probably know what I mean. When major events unfold so rapidly in your life, there's just not enough time to step back and identify your thoughts and emotions, much less process them. That's how it was for me. I obviously had concerns for my health, but I also was concerned for Judy and my family, as well as for the ministry.

In the space of three weeks—Monday, March 13 to Monday, April 3, 1995—doctors not only discovered two malignant tumors in my body, but I underwent radically invasive surgeries to remove them. How quickly plans for the immediate future can change!

I have a much deeper appreciation of the passage from James that says, *"Come now, you who say, 'Today or tomorrow, we shall go to such and such a city, and spend a year there and engage in business and make a profit.' Yet you do not know what your life will be like tomorrow. You are just a vapor that appears for a little while and then vanishes away. Instead, you ought to say, 'If the Lord wills, we shall live and also do this or that'"* (James 4:13–15).

The anesthesia contributed to my foggy memory also. Although I didn't especially fear the surgery itself, I didn't like the thought of being put under general anesthesia. One reason is that I would be totally out of control at that point. Another reason is having to deal with so many potential side effects, including nausea, which I absolutely hate. Perhaps more than any other health problem, I dread nausea. But for me, there was the additional risk of my previous heart history. After all, the cancer surgeries could go perfectly, and I could still die from complications with my heart.

It's no small thing to be wheeled away to surgery. I had to face my concerns, and one of them was the possibility of going under general anesthesia, only to wake up in the presence of the Lord. As the gospel hymn goes, "That will be glory for me," but it's still a sobering thought for those I would leave behind.

When I told my family good-bye, I knew I might not see them again in this lifetime. Let me hasten to say that most of the time patients have few real complications from anesthesia, and the vast majority of people return to reasonably good health—minus a few parts, of course.

One anecdote about my surgeries is that a good friend and a member of my board of directors, Dr. Larry Hyde of Ft. Smith, Arkansas, came to Atlanta to be with me during both of the surgeries. After conferring with my physicians and the hospital administration, he received permission to observe the procedures in the operating room.

The amusing part is that Dr. Hyde is a retired obstetrician. So the word went out that Larry Burkett had his own private obstetrician with him during the surgeries. That probably made about as much sense as anything else during that nightmare. In fact, Dr. Hyde says that one day he's going to write a book entitled *Every Husband Needs a Gynecologist He Can Trust.*

THE PRAYERS OF MY PASTOR AND CHURCH LEADERS

In the days prior to my first surgery, my pastor Jim Austin and some leaders from my church family, Blackshear Place Baptist Church, came by my office to pray with me. Following the teaching of James 5:13–16, they anointed me with oil, laid hands on me, and prayed for my healing and God's protection over my life, for which I will always be thankful.

When the church members came and prayed for me, they did not necessarily pray for a supernatural healing—a nonmedical removal of tumors. Obviously, God knew my heart and theirs as well. That's what we all desired from a personal perspective. But I asked them to pray for God's will, not mine. If, for the higher glory of God, I was to suffer through these two surgeries and through the subsequent pain and recovery, I was willing to do that.

It has been clearly established that God's will, not ours, changes the lives of others, as I'll share with you later in this book. There have been events during the last year or so since my surgeries that have confirmed this fact to me over and over again: *It was God's will that I go through not only the surgeries and the recoveries but also through a series of alternative therapies that may well be of benefit to other cancer sufferers in the future.*

Among the church leaders who prayed with me was Dr. Bill White, who remained when the others left. He said, "Larry, I would like to share something with you. A good friend of mine has been diagnosed with cancer, and he has a particularly virulent form called melanoma. His doctor gave him only a few months to live. His son, who is very much of a nutritionist, started looking all over the world for any treatments that might help. After careful research, they settled on one in Prague in the Czech Republic."

Bill went on to explain generally what the treatment involved. Basically, it consisted of an immune boosting therapy that was available only in Prague. I will honestly confess how little I knew about my immune system at the time. I knew everyone has one, that it's supposed to help fight off diseases, and that something was obviously wrong with mine.

I deeply appreciated Dr. White's comments. They helped me to begin thinking about what treatments I would pursue after the surgeries if, indeed, I survived them both.

As an aside, Dr. White and I have gotten to be very good friends over the last year, and we've spent many hours together, with our wives, talking about alternative therapies and traditional medicine and how both apply to our lives. All too often, we have the tendency to think if we aren't doing something here in America, then it can't be done, and that's simply not true. Doctors in other nations are doing excellent research also.

Another tidbit about Dr. White: He also happens to be a retired OB-GYN. It would seem that the Lord's plan for me is not to have just one personal obstetrician, but perhaps two. I'm not exactly sure what that's supposed to mean, but I'm not willing to sit down and try to figure it out either.

ROUND ONE: REMOVING MY RIGHT KIDNEY

Monday morning, March 20, 1995 arrived, along with my trip to the operating room to have my right kidney removed.

The procedure itself lasted for nearly four hours, I'm told, and it was completed without a hitch. The results came in a "good news-bad news" format. The bad news was that the tumor was definitely renal cell carcinoma, as the doctors had suspected all along. Once the kidney was removed, they were able to confirm the malignancy. The good news was the lack of any other detectable cancer in the tissues surrounding the kidney.

Sometimes I wonder about modern medicine. Surgeons tend to

overdo. For instance, a kidney is not a very big organ. It's only five or six inches long and two or three inches across. But after the operation I discovered that my incision went from about one inch shy of my navel to about an inch and one-half shy of my backbone.

So I asked my doctor the obvious: "Why did you have to cut fourteen or fifteen inches just to remove a six-inch organ from my body?"

He responded, "Well, we wanted to look around inside and see how the other organs in your body were doing; and, in fact, they're doing quite well."

Little did I know at that time that the surgery, called a radical nephrectomy, would cause me great grief over the next year. It seems that one of the primary nerves from the area of incision got trapped inside the scar tissue and it became inflamed. As a consequence, it has hurt ever since.

Subsequently, I used the services of a pain doctor who's been treating the nerve, trying to make it work properly. When she injected me with a local anesthetic, the pain abated—at least temporarily. Unfortunately, on a second visit, when a more permanent pain deadener was used, it failed. In fact, it resulted in even greater pain. But once a decision is made and the die is cast, we have to learn to live with it and not look back, second guessing ourselves.

BE CAREFUL WHAT YOU SAY

I would like to make a point here: Christians can mean well and yet say some of the most inappropriate things at the wrong time. Before you make remarks to someone recovering from cancer surgery (or any other illness, for that matter), think about how your words will impact the other person. Proverbs 16:24 says, *"Pleasant words are a honeycomb, sweet to the soul and healing to the bones."* On the other hand, harsh words can cause grief to the soul.

In one instance, the day following the first surgery I was deep in thought, obviously concerned about this new episode in my life and trying to sort out my options. Normally a family tries to screen visitors, especially if the patient is not having a good day and just doesn't feel up to having company. That's what Judy and my family were doing for me that day, but somehow a young man managed to get in to see me.

He approached my bedside, introduced himself, and then said, "Larry, I'm a renal cell carcinoma patient also, and you might as well face it: You're going to die. I'm going to die and you are too, because there just isn't any cure for this type of cancer."

Frankly, I don't know what else he said. I stopped listening to him, and Judy quickly led him from the room. He may have had the best of intentions and genuinely thought he was helping me when, in fact, he offered only words of discouragement. Very likely, he was simply venting his own anger and frustration, and I was available. But whatever his reason, it was totally inappropriate. I didn't need him to tell me the inevitable consequence of kidney cancer. I already had been informed of that possibility, and I did not need his counsel at that moment in time.

As a word of encouragement, let me say something else: Every person is different and what works for one may not work for another. Don't get discouraged and give up. If you do you probably *will* die. Attitude and determination are more than half of any recovery.

Later, I had a visit from another well-meaning friend whose wife had died from renal cell carcinoma—the same cancer I had—and had just been buried *that day.* As you might imagine, he was still in shock and was grief-stricken and needed to share with somebody. Unfortunately, he told me about the excruciating pain his wife had suffered during the last three years of her life and described all the trauma they had endured. I didn't need to hear that!

Be careful what you say when you visit friends or family in the hospital. Ask God to help you understand what the patient may be experiencing, as well as how you can be an *encouragement.*

Sometimes the most appropriate thing may be just to pray and leave.

Under no circumstances should you suggest that those who are suffering are doing so because of some sin or because of a lack of faith or because of any personal theology you may espouse. When in doubt, keep quiet! And, by all means, don't mention the potentially severe consequences of their illness. Be positive in what you say to any patient. The Holy Spirit does the work of convicting of sin (see John 16:8).

TOO MUCH TOO FAST

As I look back on that time period of the two weeks between my first and second surgery, I think of how naive I was about recuperation. I never had been hospitalized and, unfortunately, often had prided myself on the fact that I was healthy. Somehow, after my first surgery I felt like I had to get up and prove that I was going to be okay—not necessarily to anyone else but certainly to myself. I felt that God had given me a different body than the average person, that it would recover better, and that I would be able to go right back to doing what I had done before.

So within two days of returning home, I was up and walking regularly. I had accustomed myself to walking four or five miles a day before the operation and, therefore, I was still in pretty good shape. In my recuperation, I was not able to walk four or five miles, but I did walk at least a half mile. I look back on that now and wonder if, in fact, I did damage to my body because what it really needed was to recover. Unfortunately, sometimes ego and pride get in the way, and they interfere with the natural healing process that God desires for us.

Other than that, my recuperation went surprisingly well. I left the hospital within four days, and although I did have some pain it was manageable. I took pain medication for only three days following the surgery, in spite of the fact that I looked like *JAWS* had taken a bite out of me.

PRAYERS MAKE A DIFFERENCE

I cannot overstate how much it meant to know that God's people were praying for me. I could literally feel their prayers. I could sense God's hand upon me. I can attest to the peace of God that surpasses our understanding, because during what could have been (and perhaps should have been) one of the most traumatic times in my life, I had a sense of peace that truly surpassed all my understanding.

Though God didn't remove the tumors supernaturally, He certainly did provide what He promised to me, and that was His peace. I believe it came as a direct result of God's people caring and praying.

Just days before my second operation, my longtime friends, Dr. James Dobson and Mike Trout of the Focus on the Family radio program, interviewed me over the phone during their daily broadcast (on March 29, 1995). When asked how their listening audience could pray for me, I replied with four items: that God would grant my doctors mercy and grace in the upcoming surgery; that the cancer would not return; that God would sustain us in His supernatural peace; and that He would use the circumstances to draw us closer to Him.

Dr. Dobson was so comforting when he replied with these words: "Well, we sure love you, Larry, and we'll be in touch [next] Monday. We'll try to keep our listeners updated. I know you're trying to do that through your radio program too. Just know when you go in there [for the upcoming surgery] that you are literally *bathed* in prayer."

Friends. Only people last forever, and friends are so important. I praise God for the friends He has given me over the years—like the ones at Focus on the Family. Strength, peace, and encouragement are mine because of praying friends.

Within days of the operation, cards, letters, testimonies, and flowers began to flow into the ministry office. Perhaps you never know how many friends and well-wishers you have until you're down. Certainly that's how it was for me.

In the days, weeks, and months following the surgeries, Judy and I read every card and letter. I obviously couldn't read them all myself, so Judy read many of them to me. I couldn't listen to many at one time, because I would end up in tears over the faithfulness and compassion of God's people. One letter was particularly touching.

It was from a nine-year-old boy suffering from a terminal illness himself. He took the time to write and say that he had been listening to my radio programs as he lay in his bed. After hearing that I was sick also, he committed to praying for me every single day. It's hard not to see the grace of God in people when a terminally ill 9-year-old boy writes to a 56-year-old man and encourages him in the Lord.

Perhaps the thing that I remember most about these cards and letters was the compassion that God's people demonstrate for one another. I just happened to be the recipient of that compassion, and I was startled by the numbers of people who testified that they had met the Lord while listening to a radio program that dealt with personal finances. It truly has convicted me that God uses His Word in a mighty way if I will simply be a transmitter of God's Word and not an interference.

Another letter I remember was from an attorney who had accepted Christ as a result of hearing a television program that I did with Dr. John Ankerberg. During that program we discussed the economy and I quoted several verses from the Bible that dealt with economics. The attorney was so irritated by what I said that he began drafting a letter to the FCC to demand that they do something to keep religious "kooks" like me off the air.

To verify his point, the attorney wrote down all the Scriptures I had quoted—just to demonstrate how blatantly I had abused them. In the process of looking them up, however, God so convicted him that what I said was correct that he committed his life to Christ! The man is now serving the Lord full-time.

In situations like that, it certainly is not me or anyone else who makes it happen. We don't produce conversions; that is the work of the Holy Spirit. God was calling that attorney to Him at that point in time.

God wants each of us to be faithful witnesses and to trust Him for the results. I just happened to be voicing the right words for God to reach this man. As I said, there were thousands of notes and letters, each of which was a special blessing.

At the end of the tenth day I was facing another surgery—the second would be worse than the first.

ROUND TWO: REMOVING MY LEFT SHOULDER BLADE

I quickly learned that the medical term for the shoulder blade is *scapula*, and I found out what it does. For instance, when you lift your arm above your head, your scapula enables that motion. The fact that you can touch the top of your head means that your scapula is working very well.

Prior to my second surgery, the doctors explained that I would have very limited use of my left arm after my scapula was removed. A total scapulectomy is a very rare procedure. In fact, the doctors could only document about one hundred of these operations in the entire twentieth century. Thus, there were no replacement scapulas available.

Two weeks to the day after my kidney surgery I went back to the operating room, this time for removal of my left scapula. In one of the earlier meetings with the doctors, I suggested doing *both* surgeries at the same time. They both laughed and said, "You can't do that, Larry. Number one, they're on different sides of your body—one's on the right and the other's on the left. So we can't do them simultaneously. And number two, we wouldn't want to keep you under anesthetic long enough to do both of the operations anyway."

Praise the Lord they didn't follow my suggestion and do both surgeries on the same day. One at a time proved to be quite sufficient.

The scapulectomy itself went smoothly, even though it lasted nearly five hours. The aftermath was much more painful than the first surgery but, again, we had reasons for hope. The doctors could find no evidence of cancer in the surrounding tissues. Their report was, "We got it all," meaning, as far as they could tell.

In fact, the doctors were quite mystified about how the primary kidney tumor metasticized to my left shoulder but failed to spread other tumors elsewhere. Normally when a soft tissue tumor has metasticized, cancer has spread into other organs of the body.

Although some may call it coincidence, I believe that God allowed only the amount of cancer that was necessary to perform His perfect will in my life. Apparently at that time, it was not God's will for me to die from cancer.

I try not to focus on *why* something happens; rather, I focus on what God wants me to *do* as a result of it. I still can't say why God allowed this to come into my life, but I do believe that I have a better picture now than I did before.

Basically I believe God allowed this in my life for my own benefit and the benefit of others. In the meantime, Judy, my family and friends, and I are deeply thankful for God's provision. Like King David, I can honestly say, *"The Lord is the portion of my inheritance and my cup; Thou dost support my lot. The lines have fallen to me in pleasant places; indeed, my heritage is beautiful to me"* (Psalm 16:5–6).

I CAN'T BELIEVE WHAT I DID!

Feeling like I do about hospitals, I wanted to get in and out as soon as possible. So the second day following the shoulder operation I told my doctors I was in good shape, I wasn't having any significant pain, and I didn't need to be hooked up to the pain medication machine any longer. I probably exaggerated a little bit, thinking I could hasten my release from the hospital. That proved to be a huge mistake.

Two hours after they unhooked me from the epidural pain control machine, I began to hurt. I mean *really* HURT. By that time, however, it was too late. The nurse explained that they could not put me back on the machine again. Instead, I had to take oral pain relievers, and they weren't *nearly* as effective.

The next few days were particularly painful, and they got worse due to an inadvertent mistake of the nursing staff. Apparently not realizing that I had gone through the removal of my right kidney—only two weeks before, they put a pull-up bar over my bed. With my left arm incapacitated, I could only pull myself up with my right arm—the same side as my kidney surgery.

The first time I tried to pull myself up, I felt a little "pop" in my right side. Later I realized I had probably created a surgical hernia by pulling on the stitches much too soon. Whatever the medical explanation, I can tell you it hurt. Major pain on my right side; major pain on my left side. Even though I have a relatively high threshold of pain, it was exceeded.

A GODLY SPOUSE

What a blessing from the Lord a godly spouse is in time of need. Judy was right there at my side. There was very little that she could do to actually relieve my suffering. But with her at my side, I felt like there were two of us fighting this thing and not just me alone.

She rarely left the hospital, before or after either surgery. No amount of coercion on my part or anybody else's could get her to leave. We've been married for thirty-eight years now, and she's invested far too much in our relationship to let me die without her around. And she wasn't about to leave me in the hands of a hospital staff who might spoil me. No way!

In another little aside story, after I had my heart attack back in 1990, I decided to do some of the things I had always wanted to do, but never got around to them. One of those activities was learning to snow ski (growing up in Florida had not allowed for snow skiing). So we traveled to my brother's place in Steamboat Springs, Colorado about six months after my angioplasty for my very first ski experience. Judy was right there with me. She never left my side on the slopes, even for a minute, for fear that I would die learning to ski. Not only did I not die, I learned to ski in the process, and I loved it!

ALONE WITH THE LORD

Five days after my left shoulder blade was removed, I was released from the hospital. I quickly learned that, along with the shoulder blade, the doctors also removed all the muscle tissue that was attached to the underside of the scapula. Those muscles enable the truly remarkable movements your shoulder is capable of.

Everything became an effort. It was an effort to sit up. It was an effort to move. Every day presented a new battle with pain. Sleep was elusive. I was so fatigued that I'd doze off, only to be awakened by the intense pain. And with no more surgeries looming, the reality of it all began to set in and, frankly, I found myself at one of the lowest points in my life.

I found myself getting depressed as I viewed the future. The combination of still facing a future with cancer, as well as a significant disability, began to weigh me down. But, precisely when things seemed dimmer than ever, I began to sense a new work of God's Spirit in my life.

When all the visitors left and family members had fallen asleep, the house was completely quiet. I was alone with the Lord. In our hectic society, total silence is a rare commodity. I would simply clear my mind and allow God to direct my thoughts. During these times, especially when I couldn't sleep, I read my Bible, studying familiar passages but discovering new meaning in them.

Perhaps when you're battling a terminal illness God gives a special grace to understand His written Word more clearly. Passages that spoke of God's desire to draw near to me for fellowship were particularly encouraging, along with verses that talked about life after death and the fact that our eternal reward is with the Lord. Romans 8:18 reminded me that what I was enduring was not worthy of all that God had in store for me.

The late evenings became a special time of fellowship with the

Lord. I didn't need anyone else around to keep me company. It's not that I didn't appreciate the love and support of my family, because I did. But it was enough for me to be alone with the Lord to discover new depths of His love and grace. The following are some passages that were especially comforting to me.

"*Draw near to God and He will draw near to you*" (James 4:8). Through the intensity of my suffering, I began to draw near to God in a deeper way. I'm not quite sure how to completely describe it. It's not that I haven't been close to the Lord in previous times in my life. I have been. But stripped of personal wants, wishes, and desires, I began to sense the nearness of His presence in a deeper, richer way.

I came to a new level of appreciation for the agony that Jesus went through in His trial and crucifixion for me and for you. My pain helped me to comprehend more of His pain. "*And in the early morning, while it was still dark, He arose and went out and departed to a lonely place, and was praying there*" (Mark 1:35).

When the tragic news that John the Baptist had been beheaded reached Jesus, Matthew's gospel records the following response from Jesus. "*Now when Jesus heard it, He withdrew from there in a boat, to a lonely place by Himself*" (Matthew 14:13).

And of course, I couldn't forget how Jesus spent the night of His betrayal. Even when His closest friends on earth slept, Jesus labored before His Father in heaven in this manner. "*And He withdrew from them about a stone's throw, and He knelt down and began to pray, saying, 'Father, if Thou art willing, remove this cup from Me; yet not My will, but Thine be done.' And being in agony He was praying very fervently; and His sweat became like drops of blood, falling down upon the ground*" (Luke 22:41–42, 44).

If you want to pursue an interesting Bible study, trace how God worked in the lives of His people when He interrupted their plans and lifestyles. I recall the trials of Moses, John the Baptist, Joseph, Paul, the disciples, the prophets Habakkuk and Amos; and the list goes on.

THE MINISTRY OF LATE NIGHT CHRISTIAN RADIO

I've always been a late night person anyway, but sleep was particularly hard to come by in the weeks following my surgeries. As I lay awake because the pain prohibited sleep, one of the great blessings for me personally was to turn on my local Christian radio station and listen to the comforting music.

With so much time on my hands, I really began to focus in on the music—probably more than any other time in my life. I was amazed at how much Christian music truly centers on the theme of the death and resurrection of Jesus Christ. And not only His resurrection that took place some 2,000 years ago, but *our* resurrection—the future for those who trust Jesus Christ as Lord and Savior—to eternal life. What a comfort that message was, reasserting that death is not a curse but a reward—for God's people.

In retrospect, I was intrigued by the way God had switched the ministry tables on me. For years, He had opened the door for me to minister to others over the airwaves. Now I was being ministered to in a mighty way by the same medium of ministry: Christian radio.

I was experiencing one of the very stewardship principles that I had so often taught: *"At this present time your abundance being a supply for their want, that their abundance also may become a supply for your want, that there may be equality; as it is written, 'HE WHO gathered MUCH DID NOT HAVE TOO MUCH, AND HE WHO gathered LITTLE HAD NO LACK'"* (2 Corinthians 8:14–15).

Let me interject right here an unsolicited commercial for Christian radio. I've been involved with Christian radio now for about fifteen years and I find that it is crucial to contact God's people throughout the world. You know, in great part, Christians don't own a string of newspapers or television stations, but we do have an enormous number of Christian radio stations throughout America. They are the best resource available to God's people to communicate quickly with one another and as a means of ministering to each other.

I pray that God's people will protect the medium of Christian radio as a sacred trust from the Lord. That means if you listen to Christian radio, you should support it. If it is a nonprofit, non-commercial station, send a donation. If it is a commercial station, buy advertising on that station and encourage others to advertise as well. If we ever lose access to Christian radio, there will be a great gap in spreading the Gospel across the world. End of commercial!

THE ROAD TO RECOVERY

About a week or so after my second surgery, I returned to Emory University Hospital for a check-up and to get the staples removed from my shoulder. While I was there, I had an appointment to see my urological oncologist, Dr. Graham, who specializes in cancer of the urinary tract.

After his exam, he shared a very sobering statistic with me: Only some 20 percent of renal cell carcinoma patients who had a metastasis like I did survive more than two years, and only a small fraction survive more than five years.

Once my kidney and tumor had been removed, he explained, there were very few treatments available for renal cell carcinoma, and most of those didn't work very well. Traditional chemotherapy would be of no virtual value to me; and, unless I had an isolated tumor, let's say on my spine or arm or leg, radiation wouldn't be of much value. In fact, when renal cell carcinoma is exposed to radiation, although the tumors do shrink back, they very rarely ever disappear. So, essentially, I was looking at a cancer for which there is no treatment, outside of surgery, and virtually no cures anybody knows of.

The next logical question I asked Dr. Graham was, "What do we do next?"

"Wait," he said. "There's nothing else to do. If something else shows up in your body, then we will aggressively try to treat that. In the meantime, you just have to wait."

In truth, I don't wait very well when given a choice. I felt this was like asking a skydiver who had just jumped out of an airplane without a parachute to wait and see if he could land on something soft when he hit the ground. Possible, but the chances aren't very good. If I were that skydiver without a parachute, I suspect I would at least begin flapping my arms. It may not help, but at least I'd have the satisfaction of doing something. I felt the same way about waiting to see if the cancer reappeared.

Weak as I was physically, I left the doctor's office that day with a renewed determination to find some type of proactive treatment—something that I could do to strengthen my body's war against the reappearance of cancer cells.

CHAPTER SIX

Do You Really Trust God?

Facing the possibility of death brought an instant and intense focus to my life. News of a serious illness tends to do that. God's Word plainly tells us that we are destined to die. *"It is appointed for men to die once and after this comes judgment"* (Hebrews 9:27).

Job also had something to say. *"Since his days are determined, the number of his months is with Thee, and his limits Thou hast set so that he cannot pass. . . .Man dies and lies prostrate"* (Job 14:5,10).

Like many people, I have thought through the message of eternal life in Jesus Christ many times. That message of Good News is inextricably threaded throughout the Gospel of Jesus Christ and is the focus of many sermons in church pulpits, especially around Easter.

But the reality that I could die—realistically within a few months to a year—brought new meaning to some old teaching. The thoughts of facing death in the near future caused me to examine my faith. I had to answer the question, "Do I *really* trust God? Or have I just been *saying* that I trust Him?" I think such a self-examination is both normal and healthy.

In fact, the apostle Paul encouraged this kind of introspection. *"Test yourselves to see if you are in the faith; examine yourselves! Or do you not recognize this about yourselves, that Jesus Christ is in you— unless indeed you fail the test?"* (2 Corinthians 13:5).

In addition to being self-motivated, several other events triggered a deeper review of my faith in Jesus Christ.

THE MATTER OF UNCONFESSED SIN

I received thousands of cards and letters from God's people during this time—literally boxes filled to overflowing, for which I will always be grateful. (See chapter 13 for a small portion of those.) Most of the messages were very supportive and comforting, but not all were so positive.

For instance, one well-intentioned man wrote, "Larry, God has led me to write you about your illnesses. Over the last several years, you seem to have had several health-related problems. If you would simply confess the hidden sins in your life, God would heal you of these, because it's His desire that none of His children be ill." Obviously this man meant well but, in truth, he was being rather sanctimonious. I'm sure there are people who are sick because of some unconfessed sins in their lives, but that's not always the case. It is not even the norm.

The most obvious example I can think of is the apostle Paul. According to 2 Corinthians 12, Paul had some type of physical ailment that inhibited his ministry to some degree. He prayed three times that God might remove it and, in effect, God told him,

"Paul, it is for your benefit that you have this illness." From that point on, Paul no longer prayed for God to heal him physically, as far as we know.

Bear in mind that the apostle Paul had laid hands on many people and had seen them miraculously healed by God's power and, yet, he could not heal himself. Why? Because God wanted Paul to know that He was the apostle's total resource—not his body, his intelligence, or his education. So although I'm sure there are people who are ill because of unconfessed sin, only God can judge that.

I personally believe there are at least four reasons why people become ill.

First, we live in aging bodies in a fallen world, which results in sickness and suffering. If I drive my car long enough, I know the parts must eventually be replaced, and the same is true with our bodies. Replacing body parts is more difficult, however, and eventually our bodies will be overcome (unless the Lord returns first!).

Second, some people get sick because of sinful behavior which is, in fact, harmful to their bodies. In these instances, people need to confess their sins, repent of unholy behavior, and ask God's forgiveness.

Third, God allows an illness to come upon people for the benefit of the kingdom of God. I believe that was true in Paul's case. In my opinion Joni Eareckson Tada is also an example of that. Obviously God didn't cause her injury, but He allowed it because He knows when even a sparrow falls to the ground. Obviously God knew that Joni was strong enough to bear up under that burden and use it as a witness for the Lord Jesus Christ, which she has done marvelously.

Fourth, note that God sometimes allows Satan to buffet Christians to determine the caliber of their faith. The clearest example of that in Scripture is Job. Through no apparent fault of his own, Job was afflicted both with physical problems—being covered with boils—and with nonphysical problems—the loss of his children and wealth. Yet we know that these problems were for the glory of God, because the millions of people who have lived since Job remember him as a godly example of suffering and faith. Why? Because he was willing to accept God's plan for his life.

So I encourage Christians to be very careful about telling other people that they suffer because of unconfessed sin. Perhaps they do, but that's not always true. Remember Christ's admonition: *"How can you say to your brother, 'Brother, let me take out the speck that is in your eye,' when you yourself do not see the log that is in your own eye? You hypocrite, first take the log out of your own eye, and then you will see clearly to take out the speck that is in your brother's eye"* (Luke 6:42).

The idea that no Christian should ever be sick or experience any kind of problem, financial or otherwise, except as the result of unconfessed sin, is not biblical, and it comes very close to heresy.

I don't know exactly why these physical afflictions came upon me; but, I do know that my relationship with God is right, and as long as He leaves me on this earth I will praise Him, regardless of the circumstances around me—or in me. And I can tell you truthfully, I appreciate Christians who say, "We pray for you, brother, and we love you" much more than I do those who say, "Larry, you obviously have some secret, unconfessed sin in your life somewhere, and if you'll be honest before God and confess it God will heal you."

That is not what you need to hear when you're already beaten down with pain and physical problems and you know that, to the best of your ability, you've confessed any and all sins to God.

IS CANCER A PUNISHMENT FROM GOD?

As I examined my personal faith in God, another issue I had to work through was whether or not God was disciplining me through cancer. This issue was pretty closely related to inspecting my heart for any unconfessed sin, but it was still a distinct issue that crossed my mind in the wee hours of the mornings when I couldn't sleep. The following encounter illustrates how I resolved this issue.

Recently, at the doctor's office, I had the opportunity to share with a woman who is suffering from cancer, but she is also suffering from tremendous guilt. She is a Christian and believes she is serving God to the best of her ability. But in her younger years, she had gotten caught up in the rebellious movement of the mid-sixties and had done a lot of things she was ashamed of. She'd been into drugs and promiscuity—even into robberies from time to time. Although she never got caught or convicted, she still has great guilt over her past.

Her suffering was multiplied because she could not forgive herself. Neither could she believe that God would forgive her. As a result, her life was one of turmoil and unrelenting stress. As I talked with her, she admitted that she believed her cancer was a punishment from God for her past. The question I asked her was, "Have you confessed your past to God?"

She said, "Yes, I've confessed it to God and I've confessed it openly to my church."

I said, "Do you believe God forgave you for your past?"

She said, "Well, I used to, but when I got cancer I just assumed this was God's punishment for my past." I assured her that simply is not the case. God willingly gave up His own son on Calvary's cross to take the punishment for her sins—past, present, and future. Certainly God "allowed" her cancer because He knows about everything that happens to each of us. Probably none of us will know *why* these things happen. But I don't believe that God goes around zapping His people with disease as a reminder of their previous sins.

IS IT FAITH . . . OR PRESUMPTION?

Another theme that surfaced in the cards and letters I received suggested that my cancer would be eradicated if my faith was strong enough. These well-meaning people attempted to encourage me by saying, "Larry, if you just had enough 'faith,' God would heal you of this cancer. You've just got to believe."

This was another issue I had to consider. Was I simply deficient in faith? As I worked through this possibility, my thoughts went something like this. The underlying premise, as I understand it, is that if people have a healthy and solid faith in God, they will not experience sickness, illness, disease, or death. In a larger sense, the conclusion is that anyone who experiences these symptoms or other tragic circumstances in their lives therefore must not have enough faith.

I find that there is a very fine line between what we call faith and presumption. Faith, to me, is trusting God to do what His Word promises us, without any hedging. For instance, God's Word promises *"that if you confess with your mouth Jesus as Lord, and believe in your heart that God raised Him from the dead, you shall be saved"* (Romans 10:9). By faith we can claim that promise. That's true faith.

God's word says, *"My peace I give to you; not as the world gives, do I give to you"* (John 14:27). Paul said that God's peace will surpass your understanding, and I believe that promise by faith—even when the circumstances don't warrant it.

On the other hand, presumption commits God to move in a specific, particular manner and excludes all other possibilities. For example, in the pursuit of alternative treatments for my cancer, I met a man whose five-year-old son was suffering from advanced leukemia. The man and his wife were believers, and their particular sect believed that you should never have your child treated by a doctor. They had been taught that God does not work through any type of medicine or treatment. As a result, the child had not been treated for the leukemia. I could understand their hesitation if it was from a practical perspective—not wanting their child to undergo chemotherapy due to its devastating side-effects— but theirs was not effect-related.

In this case, the young child didn't get better; instead he became progressively worse, and by the time his parents sought treatment it was too late. There is no doubt that God could have performed a miracle and healed their child, but apparently He chose not to, because the child ultimately died. Again, I think we need to be very careful in distinguishing between what we call "faith" and what is really "presumption."

Be careful when you box God into one, and only one, way of responding. He is sovereign, meaning He is completely free to rule and act as He chooses. He is not a magical genie to be called out of an old lamp to rescue us upon command.

We also can be presumptuous with God when we conclude that only good things happen to His people. I disagree with the basic premise that bad things never happen to good people. The Bible is replete with examples of terrible things that can come upon God's people of faith and make them suffer.

Study the life of Joseph in Genesis chapters 37 through 50 and you will see an example of a godly, righteous man who chose to obey God in the midst of adversity, yet found himself suffering on many occasions.

What about the life of the apostle Paul? He was clearly God's servant, chosen to take the Gospel to the entire Gentile world; yet, 2 Corinthians 11:23–28 describes many of the calamities to which he was subjected.

Consider Jesus Himself. He came in love to save the world from sin and, instead, was rejected and brutally crucified by the very ones He came to save!

The eleventh chapter of Hebrews is sometimes referred to as "The Faith Hall of Fame"; the roll call of great saints of God is given, along with their feats. It's so refreshing and inspiring to read of these great men, until you reach the latter portion of the chapter, which surprisingly ends with this description of how God's "greatest" were treated here on earth.

"Others were tortured, not accepting their release, in order that they might obtain a better resurrection; and others experienced mockings and scourgings, yes, also chains and imprisonment. They were stoned, they were sawn in two, they were tempted, they were put to death with the sword; they went about in sheepskins, in goatskins, being destitute, afflicted, ill-treated (men of whom the world was not worthy)" (Hebrews 11:35–38).

My point is that God's people can be rock solid in their faith and, yet, still experience some rather horrific situations here on the earth. In the next chapter I intend to address *why* Christians, or anyone for that matter, suffer.

If you are building your Christian foundations on the idea that your commitment to God will automatically insulate you from suffering here on earth, you're in for a big shock. That notion fails to square with biblical and church history, including how the saints are being persecuted *right now* in different parts of the world.

I have a dear friend who recently lost his wife to cancer and both of them were trusting God to heal her. They were solid in their faith; there's no question about that. They did not demand that God supply a miraculous healing. Instead, they were looking for God to provide them with an answer to the cancer; and, as a result, they sought out every available therapy.

In the midst of their confusion and pain, another ministry leader called and assured them—*in fact, guaranteed* them—that God had told him she would not die from the cancer. And yet, she did. As a result, my friend's faith was severely shaken because he had based his hope on someone else's false prophecy. That does not make my friend a lesser or immature Christian. In fact, he is very normal, but he had allowed himself to accept a supposed "word of knowledge," rather than *the Word*.

We must always remember that God does not work for us; we work for Him. He is God the Almighty, the Omnipotent, Omniscient creator of the universe, and we are individually His creations. Remember how God chastened Job in the midst of his affliction, when He asked, *"Will the faultfinder contend with the Almighty? . . .Who has given to Me that I should repay him?"* (Job 40:2, 41:11).

We need to constantly keep that perspective in mind. My friend's faith has since stabilized and he's doing much better. He still doesn't understand why his wife died. Neither do I. We may never know; in fact, we probably won't—until we get to heaven. And when we see her there, it won't matter anyway.

Since we are not infinitely wise like God, we must yield to Him in the things we cannot understand. God is the leader, and we are His followers.

REVIEWING THE BEGINNINGS OF MY FAITH

The process of examining my personal faith in Jesus Christ ultimately led me to reflect on my conversion back in 1971. That's the bottom line. Was I *indeed* saved by God when I thought I was? Pursuing the answer to that question helped me to reconfirm my belief in the power, authority, and love of the Lord Jesus Christ.

I did not grow up in a Christian family. It wasn't that my family was anti-Christian. We were just neutral. Literally, lukewarm. Christ was never discussed in my home.

As far as I know, my father was not a Christian. My mother was but she rarely, if ever, spoke of Christ or went to church. The result was, I never really concerned myself with Jesus Christ. I wasn't an atheist though. I can remember, even as a small child, thinking that I shouldn't do anything to offend God, because He was all-powerful and it wouldn't be a good idea to have Him mad at me. But that was about it—the totality of my understanding of God.

When I got out of the Air Force, I went to work at Cape Canaveral in Florida. There were all types of people working at the Space Center at that time. Some were scientists who considered themselves atheists (an atheist believes there is no God). Some were engineers and specialists, many of whom considered themselves agnostics (an agnostic doubts there is a God but if there is He can't be known in a personal way).

And there were Christians who believed in God and sought to live the life He called them to. Some of those who called themselves Christians seemed more like religious fanatics to me; they felt their function in life was to argue for God and to uphold Him at every opportunity. I have long since found that God is quite competent and capable of defending His own reputation. That doesn't mean we shouldn't defend our faith in God—but not to the point of dogmatism. In general I find that few people are won to the Lord because they were sufficiently aggravated or irritated by Christians.

I was always interested in talking with the atheists because up until that time I had never met anybody who literally believed there was no God, no creator of the universe. I had done a pretty thorough study of evolution and the theories of Charles Darwin myself, and I concluded that it was a lot of nonsense. *There's simply not enough physical evidence to verify evolution,* I concluded.

For instance, we have lots of bones from dinosaurs, some of the largest creatures that have ever lived on the earth. In fact, we probably could fill the Los Angeles Coliseum with their bones, and yet we don't know when they appeared or why they disappeared from the earth. But the evolutionists confidently state that man evolved from a lower species, based on a total volume of bones that wouldn't even fill a fruit bowl, and most of those have been determined to be frauds. So I had long since concluded that those who believe in evolution had to swallow a larger fairy tale than I ever thought creation to be.

Unless you've worked around avid atheists, though, you may find it hard to follow their line of thinking, because they simply don't accept anything that is said or written about God. They believe God doesn't exist and no amount of logic will convince them otherwise.

I recall a statement made by William Thomas Cummings, a World War II chaplain: "There are no atheists in the foxholes." In other words, when facing imminent death, atheists will tend to challenge their own beliefs—or their lack of beliefs. During that kind of situation, most atheists are open to hear about God and about God's Son, Jesus Christ.

At the space center there were many times when we were locked in a concrete blockhouse during a launch countdown. Sometimes we would be there for days, and during the long periods of time with nothing to do there would be some intense discussions about religion or politics. I always found myself arguing for the oppressed or the underdog.

If the group was arguing against God, I would argue for Him. If the group argued for Him, I would argue against Him, in spite of the fact that deep inside I did believe there was a God. Even as a non-Christian, it seemed to me to be the height of ignorance not to believe there was an intelligent creator of this universe.

Most of my coworkers, being from secular universities, espoused a belief in evolution. However, even they admitted they had virtually no physical evidence to prove it. They didn't believe in a world that was created by a supernatural power, but since they had to believe in something they bought into evolution. Some things never change.

I recall one experiment that was done prior to the first manned lunar landings; an unmanned probe was sent to the moon. One of the popular discussions going on in academic circles was that if, in fact, the world was between five and seven billion years old, the landing pods on the lunar lander would need to be oversized to support the spacecraft. The evolutionist scientists calculated that there would be several feet of very fine cosmic dust that had settled on the moon over these eons.

If the evolutionist theory was correct, their logic made sense. We knew, based on data from previous experiments with orbiting solar panels, how frequently cosmic dust struck the panels, and thus it was possible to calculate how deep the dust would be on the moon's surface—if indeed it was between five and seven billion years old. Obviously it would be several feet.

When the probe landed on the moon, however, much to everyone's surprise, the cosmic dust proved to be only *about an eighth of an inch deep!* Rather than admitting they were wrong about the age of the earth and moon, the evolutionists concocted another explanation: "There must be more cosmic dust moving through space now than there used to be. Therefore, in the long distant past there was so little dust that it didn't accumulate much, and that's why there's only an eighth of an inch of sediment on the moon."

Well, personally, I didn't buy those mental gymnastics. True science lays all the possibilities on the table rather than sticking to one dogmatic conclusion—in this case, evolution—and twisting the evidence to fit it.

But even though I found myself arguing for God and His existence, it still never occurred to me that I could, and should, know Him personally.

WHEN SALVATION DREW NEAR

I was about 28 years old when Judy became a Christian. She was led to the Lord by some door-to-door evangelists from Campus Crusade for Christ who came to our home and presented the *Four Spiritual Laws* to her. She accepted Christ as a result of their efforts.

What's interesting is, had you asked Judy prior to this encounter if she was a Christian, she probably would have told you that she was. She had gone to church off and on most of her life, had done a lot of good things, and had even sent our kids to Christian kindergarten; but, in truth, she had never accepted Jesus Christ as her own personal Savior. The *Four Spiritual Laws* brought her spiritual condition into clear focus.

After she became a Christian I remember thinking, "That's okay. I'm for anything that will help her." After all, we had four children by this time and, like most marriages, we had our share of stress and arguments. So I was glad for Judy. But I told her that religion and church weren't for me and not to bother me with it.

Judy joined Park Avenue Baptist Church in our hometown of Titusville and, as you might imagine, over the next couple of years, the Bible "thumpers" (as I used to call them) came around to share Christ with me. But my mind was closed. I didn't want to hear it.

One of the people who came to visit me was Judy's pastor, Peter Lord. Peter is a Jamaican who moved to Florida, went to college and seminary, and became a pastor. To say that Peter has a feisty personality would be an understatement, to be sure. I remember one day when he knocked at the front door, and I thought to myself, *"Here we go again."*

Anyway, I asked Peter to come in. This was probably his third or fourth visit to our home. Our conversation quickly turned to the things of God, and we began to banter back and forth. He would say one thing and I would counter it. I remember challenging him about why he believed such "nonsense."

Peter finally became so irritated with me that he stood up and stomped out of my house, slamming the door as he went! About thirty seconds later, the door opened again, he stuck his head inside and said, "You know what, my friend? You're going straight to hell!" Then he slammed the door and left!

At the time, I chuckled about it because I didn't know much about hell, much less believe in it. I figured hell was one of those fairy tales that Christians made up to scare people into joining the church, and I wasn't about to do that.

Again, it wasn't that I didn't believe there was a God. I did. But my relationship to God was a pretty simple one. He didn't bother me and I didn't bother Him. I tried to stay out of God's way. I even knew enough about the Bible to understand the commandments of God and, as a result, I tried to never purposely violate those commandments. To the unsaved mind, the spiritual things of God are simply foolishness, and that's what they seemed to me. I believed it was a crutch that some people needed, and that was okay. After all, if it helped them, good for them! If Judy needed that crutch, that was fine with me, but I didn't need it.

DON'T COME BACK ANYMORE

Judy was pretty faithful about asking me to go to church with her, and I occasionally went to Easter or Christmas services, but that was about it. Some time later, she joined a couples' Bible study that met every Monday evening. Since it was a study for couples, she asked me if I would attend with her. It was led by a local dentist I knew, so I decided to join her.

The next few months proved to be testy. I attended the group semi-regularly and studied the Bible for the upcoming week. My purpose was to be armed and ready to argue, partially because I didn't believe what I was reading—much of it I didn't even understand—but also because it didn't appear to be true in the lives of the Christians I watched.

After a few months of this, the Bible study leader asked if I would meet him for breakfast, and I braced myself for another Gospel presentation, like so many others from the church had done. But to my surprise (and shock) that wasn't what was on his mind—at least, directly. During breakfast he said virtually nothing, but when I asked why he wanted to meet he cleared his throat and said perhaps the only thing that would break through my shell of obstinacy.

"Larry, you've obviously been reading the Bible. Right?" he asked.

"Sure," I replied. "That's like any class. You assign it and I read it. I enjoy studying."

"Well," he said, "my observation is that when you read the Bible, you read it looking for arguments."

Though I didn't say anything, I thought to myself, *Yep, that's probably true of most things I do. I want the knowledge, but something inside of me wants to challenge it.*

He continued, "I want to ask you to do two things for me. First, don't come back to my Bible study anymore. You're too disruptive and I would really prefer that you not be there with that attitude."

Needless to say, that surprised me and even irritated me a little bit. After all, my impression was that Christians normally begged people to accept Christ. I never pictured them as being confrontational, except in the heated discussions at the space center. But here sat a Christian telling me that he didn't want me to come to his Bible study. Even though it irritated me a little, I knew inside he was right.

He continued, "I want you to do something else for me, if you will. Spend some time reading the book of John; but before you do, ask God to open your heart and show you the truth. After reading John's letter, and really being honest with God about seeking the truth, if you don't see the truth there, then put the Bible down and forget about the whole thing."

And with that, he got up and left. (I think he stuck me with the breakfast bill too.)

That entire day I pondered over what he had said. Keep in mind that at this time I was a person with no *absolute* value system. I always had thought an education would make me feel fulfilled, but it didn't. Then I figured running something important would make me feel fulfilled, because I wanted to be the man in charge instead of working for someone else. By that time I was in charge, and it didn't help. Lastly, I had always thought that if I had more money, enough to be financially secure, that would make me feel fulfilled. But I knew that wouldn't bring fulfillment either.

I had long since become disillusioned with my value system. I yearned for something permanent—something absolute to believe in—but I didn't know where to look. This challenge gave me the focus I needed. That very evening I read the book of John through and through and sincerely asked God to show me the truth. And He did! He convicted me of my sinfulness, and clearly showed me that Jesus Christ really is the Son of God, and that He was sent to save me. *On September 5, 1971, my name was added to the Lamb's Book of Life.*

By that time I had heard the message of salvation so many times I could recite it by heart. Previously, when I heard the Gospel it meant absolutely nothing to me. But that particular evening, the true meaning of God's message came through—that I, Larry Burkett, was a sinner, lost and condemned to hell. By a simple acceptance of Jesus Christ as my Lord and Savior, I could have eternal life with God the Father.

In my case, at that particular time, I wasn't looking for eternal life as much as I was peace on this earth. I needed to believe in something. I needed to have some absolutes in my life. I needed to know where I was going and what I was supposed to do—what my purpose on earth was. And though I didn't understand the entire plan that evening in September, I did know that I was finally on the right track.

The Sunday after I accepted Christ I went with Judy to church. At that point she didn't know that I had asked Christ into my life. In fact, no one did. I hadn't told anyone about my decision. Though I sat through the entire church service, I'm not sure I heard a word Pastor Lord was saying. When the service came to a close, Peter asked if anybody present would like to come forward to make a confession of Christ. I got out of my seat and made my way down front. When Peter saw me coming, I think the blood drained from his face. I don't know if he thought I was coming to start a fight or what.

Finally, when we stood face to face, I shook his hand and said, "I want to announce that I accepted Jesus Christ as my Savior."

Peter literally shouted out, "Hallelujah!"

We have since developed a firm lifetime friendship. Often after that, when Peter would go out on Wednesday evenings to witness to people who were unsaved, he took me along for the "hard cases," using me as an example by saying, "If God can save this guy, He can save anybody, including you. You still have a chance."

When I asked Christ into my life, I made a commitment to God that I would never again be deliberately disobedient. I promised the Lord, "Whatever You say, I will do to the best of my ability, even if it costs me everything." I firmly believe that not only must we accept him as Savior but also as Lord; and, as Lord over our lives, He has the right to use us however *He* chooses.

I made that commitment over twenty-five years ago, and I am constantly surprised how the Lord chooses to use me. No doubt He has allowed me to experience many difficulties; but, in retrospect, the trials have had a cumulative effect of helping to strengthen my faith—not weaken it. That means learning to trust *Him* when I don't have all the answers, which is most of the time.

I don't know if cancer will take my life or if I'll die a natural death at the age of 90. Only the Lord really knows. I still can't answer *why* God has allowed cancer to come into my life, but over the past months I can tell you that I see a clearer picture of some possibilities that have surfaced.

For whatever reason, God has placed me in a position of high visibility, and it may be that God wants to use that visibility to help the faith of others. Perhaps someone with a cure for cancer will contact me and, as a result, I may be able to pass it on to others. Maybe not. Those answers are clearly in God's hands, not mine, and I try to just keep doing what God has called me to do every day, trusting that He has the big picture and will tell me what I need to know at the time when I need to know it.

HOW YOU CAN BE SURE ABOUT YOUR HEAVENLY HOME

Now that I've told you about my personal faith in Jesus Christ and how it has helped me cope with my cancer experience, I'm concerned for you. Have you committed your life to Jesus Christ? If not, what hope can you possibly have for life after death? Since we all live in mortal bodies, it is an *absolute fact* that one day our earthly bodies are going to quit. We're all in the same boat. We don't know when our departure from this life is going to take place, so the wise man or woman will be ready.

Keep in mind that since the time I was diagnosed with a very severe form of cancer, thousands of Americans have died in automobile accidents, most of whom were in good health. There are no assurances about tomorrow, so be ready.

If you have not accepted Jesus Christ as Lord and Savior, let me assure you that you're not ready to step into eternity. A righteous God will allow you to inherit an eternal home in a lake of fire and torment—*hell*—after your death. Why would a loving God do this? Because He has provided a means of atonement and you simply rejected it. Gathering from the many Bible references that speak of eternal damnation or hell, I can tell you this: You don't want to spend eternity there. By reviewing the verses below, I think you'll see what I mean.

> "But the sons of the kingdom shall be cast out into the outer darkness; in that place there will be weeping and gnashing of teeth" (Matthew 8:12).

> "And these will go away into eternal punishment, but the righteous into eternal life" (Matthew 25:46).

> "The Lord Jesus shall be revealed from heaven with His mighty angels in flaming fire, dealing out retribution to those who do not know God and to those who do not obey the gospel of our Lord Jesus. And these will pay the penalty of eternal destruction, away from the presence of the Lord and from the glory of His power" (2 Thessalonians 1:7–9).

> "And I saw the dead, the great and the small, standing before the throne, and books were opened; and another book was opened, which is the book of life; and the dead were judged from the things which were written in the books, according to their deeds. . . .And if anyone's name was not found written in the book of life, he was thrown into the lake of fire" (Revelation 20:12,15).

This is not the way God wants it to be. In fact, God gave His only Son Jesus Christ to die on the cross to rescue you from eternal separation from Him. First Timothy 2:4 says that God "desires all men to be saved and to come to the knowledge of the truth." Second Peter 3:9 clearly says that God "is patient toward you, not wishing for any to perish but for all to come to repentance."

Perhaps you've been a church member for much of your life and, in view of some terminal illness in your life or the life of a loved one, you've begun to question what will happen to you after death. God's plan is clear: He wants you to know that you can have eternal life. Listen to what He says in His Word.

"And the witness is this, that God has given us eternal life, and this life is in His Son. He who has the Son has the life; he who does not have the Son of God does not have the life. These things I have written to you who believe in the name of the Son of God, in order that you may know that you have eternal life" (1 John 5:11–13).

If you're not sure of your salvation at this point, you can be. Let me assure you there are many people who attend church regularly, who give lots of money to God's work, and who believe they are saved, based on their good works when, in fact, they're not saved at all. That fundamental question needs to be answered at this time, and the best way to answer it is to follow God's plan.

Here are the foundational truths upon which your faith in God can rest.

Believe that Jesus Christ is the eternal Son of God, and that He is both willing and able to save you from all of your sins.

"For God so loved the world that He gave His only begotten Son, that whoever believes in Him should not perish, but have eternal life" (John 3:16).

"Christ died for our sins . . . He was buried . . . He was raised on the third day, according to the Scriptures . . . He appeared to Cephas, then to the twelve. After that He appeared to more than five hundred" (1 Corinthians 15:3–6).

Confess both your sin and your need of a Savior in Jesus Christ.

"For all have sinned and fall short of the glory of God" (Romans 3:23).

"And there is salvation in no one else; for there is no other name under heaven that has been given among men, by which we must be saved" (Acts 4:12).

By faith, accept God's salvation in Jesus Christ by personally receiving Him.

"But God demonstrates His own love toward us, in that while we were yet sinners, Christ died for us" (Romans 5:8).

"But as many as received Him, to them He gave the right to become children of God, even to those who believe in His name" (John 1:12).

YOU CAN ACCEPT JESUS CHRIST AS YOUR PERSONAL LORD AND SAVIOR RIGHT NOW BY FAITH.

Since God knows your heart, He is not so much concerned with your words as He is with the attitude of your heart. The following is a suggested prayer.

"Lord Jesus, I need You. Thank You for dying on the cross for my sins. I open the door of my life and receive You as my Savior and Lord. Thank You for forgiving my sins and giving me eternal life. Take control of the throne of my life. Make me the kind of person You want me to be."

Does this prayer express the desire of your heart? If it does, pray this prayer right now, and Christ will come into your life, as He promised.[1]

Be sure you tell others of your decision. They will be able to direct you to a good church that will help you to grow in your faith.

IT'S NEVER TOO LATE

You may be thinking to yourself, "What plan can God possibly have for my life in light of my (cancer, AIDS, heart disease, or some other serious illness)?" Remember, God's number one plan is for you to be saved for eternity. It's never too late for you to accept His salvation.

But don't forget your influence on family and friends. Your positive response to Christ Jesus will be a comfort to them and may even trigger others to respond to Jesus Christ also. The key is to do what God has told you to do, and trust Him for the outcome.

---

1. Adapted from the "Four Spiritual Laws" booklet published by Campus Crusade for Christ, International.

CHAPTER SEVEN

Coping with Pain and Suffering

O ne of the inevitable consequences of cancer, as well as most other illnesses, is the virtual certainty of pain and suffering. The assault on your body by the disease itself triggers deep hurting. On top of that, the three common methods of treating cancer—surgery, chemotherapy, and radiation—all represent powerful intrusions into your body, also resulting in considerable suffering. Although I've not had the latter two, I can attest to the fact that surgery brings with it some pretty significant pain.

This past year I've gotten to know a lot about pain. I'm not saying that to get your sympathy, because I've learned to handle whatever circumstances I find myself in. Rather, I'm sharing this to help other cancer patients, especially those who have had surgery, to accept the fact that being in pain doesn't mean God has abandoned you. Remember what the apostle Paul said, "[The Lord] *has said to me, 'My grace is sufficient for you, for power is perfected in weakness'*" (2 Corinthians 12:9).

Much of the pain I'm experiencing is going to be chronic, at least for the foreseeable future. As a result of the kidney surgery, there's a scar that runs about fourteen inches, from front to back, around my right side. As I said before, I have a nerve trapped inside the scar tissue that hurts virtually all the time. I've tried a variety of treatments to ease the pain, including an attempt to block the trapped nerve. Unfortunately, in my case, it didn't help. In fact, it actually made the pain worse for several weeks.

I also have chronic pain from the scapulectomy. Any time a bone as large as the shoulder blade is removed, there's going to be a lot of cutting by the surgeons. In addition, there are many muscles attached to the scapula, and when it is removed something has to be done with those muscles. They either have to be totally resected (removed) or reattached to something else. In my case, the surgeons elected to connect several of the muscles to the rotator cuff in order to provide more stability to my shoulder and perhaps allow better use of my left arm.

As a result, I do have fairly good use of my arm across my chest, and for that I am grateful. Unfortunately, the side effect is more pain, because those muscles have to readjust to a new position that they've never held—certainly not for the previous 56 years. So they pull and tug, and that causes my back and my shoulder to ache. In a subsequent visit to my primary surgeon, Dr. Monsen, I asked him what the alternative was, to which he replied, "Amputation." I decided to stop complaining and to learn to live with the pain.

It's been a real blessing to get up in the middle of the night with severe pain, confess to the Lord my weakness, and experience the

Lord lifting my spirits—in spite of the pain. I have purposed not to take any narcotic pain medication; that's my choice. I simply can't stand the fuzzy-headed feeling that often comes as a side effect of drugs. Everyone has to make his or her own decision, but I would rather deal with the pain than with the lack of clarity from pain control medication, although I do take aspirin or the equivalent if I have been very active the previous day.

My family has been very supportive, and they understand that there are simply times when I can't do things with them because it hurts too much. They have agreed to leave me by myself and go on and do what they want to. When I can participate, I do. Some days are better than others and warm weather seems to help.

I've heard many people quote the verse from Isaiah: *"By [Jesus']* scourging *[stripes]* we are healed" (Isaiah 53:5). The meaning intended by the verse, they imply, is that I should confess that Christ has taken away all of my pain and, therefore, I no longer have any pain. Let me assure you that I have done that—not once, but many times. I have done it in earnest and I've done it by repetition. Unfortunately, at this point at least, Christ has not chosen to take away my pain.

Is that for my benefit? I have to assume so. Is it part of a natural sin-fallen world in which God created pain to tell us when we have problems in our body? Most assuredly that's true. I would caution all Christians not to fall into the trap of some of the science-based religious cults that attempt to deny the existence of our physical bodies and, thus, pain.

One of the insights I've gained is that pain and suffering are relative to each person. Not only do people have differing physical thresholds of pain, but what one person regards as suffering, the next person may dismiss altogether. For instance, when someone tells me how badly they hurt after playing tennis or golf, I am tempted to say, *"You don't even understand what suffering really is"*; but I don't. To the person who's hurting, what they're experiencing is all-important to them at that point in time. In the past I've complained about some of those same ailments myself.

Suffering is basically anything that makes us exclaim, "Oh, no, not this!" or "Oh no, not that again!" It results from any event or circumstance that wounds us deeply, whether it is physical, emotional, mental, or spiritual.

I think it's helpful to distinguish between suffering and tribulation. In the latter, we take on a problem specifically because we are Christians, perhaps even voluntarily. For example, as Christians, we've chosen to take on tribulation as a result of identifying with Jesus Christ, rather than avoiding it by denying Him. The Bible explicitly teaches that God's people will experience tribulation from the world by virtue of our relationship to Him.

"Indeed, all who desire to live godly in Christ Jesus will be persecuted" (2 Timothy 3:12).

"These things I have spoken to you, that in Me you may have peace. In the world you have tribulation, but take courage; I have overcome the world" (John 16:33).

"In this you greatly rejoice, even though now for a little while, if necessary, you have been distressed by various trials, that the proof of your faith, being more precious than gold which is perishable, even though tested by fire, may be found to result in praise and glory and honor at the revelation of Jesus Christ" (1 Peter 1:6–7).

Suffering, on the other hand, is universal to the human experience and is not directly related to being a Christian. Christians and non-Christians alike suffer in this life and, as I have said earlier in the book, being a Christian certainly does not exempt us from suffering. Whereas God is honored when we suffer for unjust causes (see 1 Peter 2:19–20), there's no inherent glory to God in suffering. You'll note that suffering was not part of God's grand design for mankind in the Garden of Eden.

For that reason, as I mentioned previously, I elected to visit a pain doctor, a person who deals specifically in the management of pain. Initially, when the doctor injected the trapped nerve in my right side with a local anesthetic, I had instant relief. I thought to myself, "Aha! We've got this problem solved!"

But when I returned the following week, the nerve was injected with an acid designed to kill it. Not only did it not work, it made the pain worse by about 100 percent! Fortunately the pain has since receded to its previous level and is gradually getting better. I have had to learn to live with some pain, the same as many others do. But you should explore your options. Many other people who have had similar treatments were helped greatly.

With regard to the pain in my shoulder, there isn't any current therapy that can help. I worked with a physical therapist for several months: Annette Humphrey, the wife of one of our staff members at Christian Financial Concepts. She was a great help to me in reaching the maximum mobility in my left arm, where the scapula was removed. But it will never be the same again—at least not without a miracle of restoration. A major portion of the shoulder structure is gone. However, using a good therapist has really helped over the long run. She designed a sling that supports my arm and makes the shoulder more immobile. As a result, the shoulder pain has been reduced.

MENTAL SUFFERING

Another dimension to the realm of human suffering is mental anguish. Generally, this suffering stems from our inner thought patterns and attitudes that surround the actual physical suffering. The black cloud of mental suffering not only affects the patient but potentially can cast a shadow over the entire family via this simple word: *worry.* "What if this happens?" or "What if that does not happen?" we ask ourselves. These are the doubts that cross our minds in the wee hours of the morning.

One's personality can play a major role in mental suffering. For instance, God created me with a dominant and decisive personality. This is neither inherently good nor bad. It's just the way I am. High D personalities (or Dominants) have the ability to absorb a lot of information, sort through it rapidly, and come to a conclusion (which is not always correct).

As with all personality types, there are strengths and weaknesses in my personality. The strength is, I'm able to look at a wide range of materials and pull insights together into a succinct format, and hence I write and teach a great deal. The weakness is that I tend to analyze everything and, all too often, concern myself about things I shouldn't.

For example, for quite a number of years, I've seen problems in the American economy and directions in our nation that deeply distress me. I see problems in the church. I see problems in our society and, more recently, I see the potential problems with my cancer. I've come to know enough honest physicians and enough people with cancer to know that there really aren't a lot of traditional treatments that are very effective.

As you might imagine, the combined impact of all these mental burdens is considerable. It's not that I'm in a position to make most of these problems go away, but I care about what's best for our nation, the church, and my family. It greatly troubles me to think about what the future will hold for my grandchildren because of the irresponsibilities of our government today.

I better understand what the apostle Paul meant when he wrote, *"Apart from such external things, there is the daily pressure upon me of concern for all the churches"* (2 Corinthians 11:28). And I realize that how people think and the attitudes they maintain can have a tremendous impact on the progress of their recovery from an illness. Mental suffering can be every bit as painful and oppressive as the actual physical suffering; sometimes it may even be worse!

I recall the story told by a friend who was a prisoner of war (POW) in Vietnam for five years. He described another POW who received no communication from his family for more than three years. His wife had been pregnant with their first child when his Vietnam tour began. He imagined the worst: she had died, or she had forgotten him.

While a POW he developed a stomach tumor, which grew to the size of a basketball; he lost weight until he was down to ninety pounds and clearly was dying. Emotionally he had given up. Then one day his captors, as a part of a new peace accord, allowed the Red Cross to deliver packages and mail from the U.S. He received dozens of undelivered packages and letters from his wife, along with progressive photos of his son's growth. Suddenly he began to get better, the tumor shrank and then disappeared, and today—twenty-five years later—he is alive and doing well. All because of his mental attitude!

Some people attempt to relieve mental suffering simply by denying the symptoms or the problem. Denial is not the same as a positive mental attitude. I have met some people with cancer who tried to deny that they even had a problem, and it cost them their lives.

Recently I talked to a friend who had a sister—a young woman—suffering from breast cancer, who had been through virtually every kind of treatment the medical community had to offer—surgery, chemotherapy, radiation, and bone marrow transplant. I offered to put the man's sister in touch with an alternative treatment center in Tennessee. They accepted, and that contact resulted in the whole family flying to the center.

I didn't think to tell them that the facility where this project was taking place was not a university hospital and, in fact, was involved in a clandestine project. In reality, the facility looked exactly like what it was: a low-budget medical clinic—very austere and very non-medical in appearance. The family was shocked when they first saw the building, apparently expecting a huge medical complex like a university hospital.

Even though the experimental therapy was being offered at no cost and had demonstrated very positive results with dozens of other cancer patients, the daughter decided to return home without being treated. Since I was taking the treatment myself at the time, I attempted to talk her into staying, but she wouldn't hear of it.

In their attempt to protect their daughter from fear and mental suffering, her parents had not leveled with her about how bad her condition really was. Without her knowing it, the doctors had estimated she would only live another three or four months. The parents had chosen to shelter her from this, but I might add that the daughter really didn't want to know. In fact, she'd never attended a meeting with her family doctor or her oncologist, electing instead to leave that to her parents.

Her denial of her illness was quite powerful. "I'm not like those other people in there," she told me as she left the facility. "They're all sick, but I'm not. I'm doing fine. I don't need to be here."

Of course, it wasn't my place to argue with the young woman. But here is a classic case of a family locked in denial over a major illness. By trying to protect their daughter from the truth, the parents greatly multiplied their own mental anguish and postponed her taking responsibility for her own health.

My encouragement to any cancer patient is, do not deceive yourself. Walk in the truth. A positive attitude is always helpful and encouraging, but not when cloaked in denial. Facing mental pain and suffering requires great courage, but in the end, truthfulness and trust in God are the most healthy methods of coping.

EMOTIONAL SUFFERING

Whereas mental suffering revolves around our attitudes and thought patterns, emotional suffering reflects the pain we experience in our feelings. I should point out that all of the dimensions of suffering—physical, mental, emotional, and spiritual—are all very closely interconnected. For the sake of discussion, however, it's easier to focus on one aspect at a time.

I have suffered emotionally since the initial diagnosis. In our culture, many equate emotional struggles with spiritual weakness or even mental disturbances. As in the case with physical illness, it's always a possibility that emotional struggles can be rooted in some issues of sin, but it's too simplistic—and just plain wrong—to say that's always the case.

The vast majority of human beings struggle from time to time with depression. We call it "feeling blue," or "being down." Some of the great saints of the Bible struggled with these same kinds of feelings. Read about Elijah in 1 Kings 19 or about Moses in Numbers 11. Or can we read through the Psalms without hearing the pain and despair in King David's heart from time to time?

The difference between then and now is the way the church, in general, condemns or makes the battle against depression a moral issue. As I said before, depression, which is often the way emotional suffering is manifested, may or may not have moral or spiritual roots to it. As a matter of fact, most people who battle some type of physical illness know how hard it is to battle depression.

Sometimes mood swings, depression, and prolonged emotional suffering have chemical imbalances as the source. After all, some people do suffer from chemical imbalances. Along these lines, however, I must point out how hypercritical our Christian society is sometimes. For the people who suffer from a pancreatic deficiency of insulin (we call them diabetics), most Christians would heartily recommend that diabetics take insulin injections to keep their bodies healthy. Or if someone has been suffering from a thyroid deficiency, leaving him or her feeling very lethargic, the vast majority of Americans (Christians included) would tell that person to take a thyroid supplement. That only makes common sense.

But if someone experiences mood swings, depression, or prolonged emotional suffering of some sort, few would recommend medication as part of that person's solution. It's too easy to say, "Well, you just need to pray more," or "You *must* have some hidden, unconfessed sin *somewhere* in your life." Such comments usually provoke more guilt, shame, or inadequacy, which only exacerbates the problem, leaving the person in an even deeper tailspin. Heaping on more guilt does not constitute a blessing to someone struggling with emotional pain. Another common attitude that greets people with emotional struggles is "Tough it out. Learn to live with it."

I'm here to tell you that God expects more out of His church than those kinds of responses. Emotional pain and suffering are very real, and rather than helping people see God as their merciful Father, eternally filled with compassion and care, often our responses simply drive people further away from God by heaping on guilt and shame. But the Scriptures indicate that God desires for us to draw near to Him in our time of need.

"The righteous cry and the Lord hears, and delivers them out of all their troubles. The Lord is near to the brokenhearted, and saves those who are crushed in spirit" (Psalm 34:17–18).

I have had to deal with mood swings in my life, particularly following my surgeries, and on occasion I take a medication supplement to help. Although my general approach is to avoid the use of as much medication as possible for any reason, if I need the help that medication can bring, I take it. I don't need to apologize for it or even explain it. I've prayed about it and God has given me a peace about it, and that's all there is to it. You may feel differently and, if so, that's fine. I'm just saying, don't judge other people by your standards unless you are *sure* your standards are God's (see Matthew 7:1–2).

I have a friend who has a daughter in her mid-20s who suffers from significant mood swings and panic attacks, to the point that she is significantly debilitated. She's fearful of everything—fearful of dying, fearful of *not* dying, fearful of losing everything, fearful of her husband walking out on her, and it goes on and on. Each time she experiences one of these attacks, which begin with severe depression and end in panic, they build upon each other and get worse.

I asked the mother, "Has she ever tried medication to control these mood swings?" The mother was obviously taken back by my suggestion. Aghast might be a better word.

She replied, "What do you mean?"

I said, "Well, there are some drugs available through your doctor—pretty effective drugs—that have helped others control the very same symptoms. Perhaps they could help your daughter."

"Oh, no," replied the mother, "my daughter couldn't take those things. Those are *drugs*." I was surprised at the mother's response, particularly since she was a nurse.

"Don't you dispense medications to patients in your work?" I asked.

"Oh, yes."

"Well, do you give drugs to Christians as well?"

"I'm sure some of them are Christians."

"Well," I said, "do you think those Christians are unspiritual because they take the medications?"

"Of course not, Larry," she retorted. "They need them at the time."

"That's precisely my point," I countered. "The same principle applies. Don't you think your brain is an organ of the body, just like your heart and your liver and your lungs and your kidneys? Just because the brain is the reasoning area of your body doesn't mean that it cannot experience chemical imbalances like any other part of your body. It's a physical thing. Our spirits are supernatural, but our bodies are natural. Why don't you take your daughter to a doctor, have her evaluated, and see if the doctor can't prescribe some medication to help level out her emotions?"

The mother took my advice, and after several months of medical treatment, the young woman is no longer experiencing the wild emotional mood swings. Sure, there are still times when she's moody; who hasn't experienced that? But the good news is, she is functional again. She can get on with her life. What I'm saying is what I believe: If someone needs medicine to help reestablish a chemical balance in his or her brain, there's nothing immoral or unspiritual about that.

LIVING WITH PAIN

Suffering began when Adam and Eve rebelled against God by eating the forbidden fruit, and it's been a part of human experience ever since. You and I are living in a world that will yield both good and bad times. By concentrating on the good times during the bad times, you can get past the problems, past the suffering, even past the pain. All too often our Christian friends, even our pastors, in their zeal to make Christianity seem like a magic potion for every affliction, have painted a picture of the Christian life that doesn't exist.

Life as a Christian is not one of uninterrupted success or of uninterrupted good health. And it's certainly not always a life of abundant material prosperity or delightful experiences all the time. If that is true, then there are a whole lot of missionaries, prophets, and evangelists who have missed out in their lives, including the apostles.

The truth of the matter is that "More Christians were martyred last year than in the first century: 156,000." Michael Horowitz of the Hudson Institute in Washington says, "We're talking . . . about . . .persecution of the worst sort: slavery, starvation, murder, looting, burning [and] torture."[1]

One of the benefits of suffering is that it establishes your credibility as a witness for Christ. You've heard that old cliché about walking a mile in another person's shoes. I certainly can attest to that. I wouldn't choose cancer for anybody else on the face of the earth, but as a result of having it myself I have a great deal more compassion in sharing with others who do have cancer than I ever could have had otherwise.

In particular, I can speak to Christians who are down, bitter, and complaining about everything bad happening to them. Prior to my experience with cancer, I wouldn't have been able to say to them, "You know, maybe what you're doing is looking too much at yourself, focusing too much on your needs and not enough on the needs of the others around you. Perhaps you would be helped by concentrating more on the needs of the body of Christ and the unsaved world around us. Sure, you're suffering with cancer, but that doesn't exempt you from being a witness or servant for God. And the fact is, some of your friends are going to spend eternity in Hell, and you're in a position to do something about that—but not unless you get beyond your private pity party."

Now that I've had cancer, I can say those things. I'm an insider. Pain and suffering? "Been there, done that. Got the bumper sticker. Even have the T-shirt!" With confidence, I can assure you that you can be a witness for Jesus Christ *in spite of* your medical condition.

I have found that there's a certain comradeship among those battling cancer. We all feel what the other person is feeling—not so much the pain or the suffering as the understanding of the mental struggle and the change in personality that accompany cancer.

That common bond often presents a wonderful opportunity to witness for the Lord, both to the people who are suffering and also to their loved ones who are watching but don't know what to do or say. Perhaps in your case, you will be the only person who can share the Gospel with them.

"But sanctify Christ as Lord in your hearts, always being ready to make a defense to everyone who asks you to give an account for the hope that is in you, yet with gentleness and reverence" (1 Peter 3:15).

When Peter was inspired by the Holy Spirit to say *"always,"* I think that's exactly what God meant to say: always . . . even if you have cancer or some other terminal illness. Live in such a way that others can detect the hope that is within you, and then be prepared to tell the reasons behind your hope. Perhaps that means deliberately being a little bit happier than those around you. Don't be phoney about it; just ask God to grant you joy and peace in your affliction.

If you have questions to ask, then ask them. I encourage people to ask me, "How do you feel about this or that? What kind of fears do you have? What's the pain like? What do you see for your future? What do you expect? How are you doing your long-range planning? What have you done about your will? What about your estate? What have you done to prepare Judy and your family in the event you don't survive the cancer?" and questions like that. Those are legitimate and honest questions, and family and close friends should have the freedom to ask them.

Let God's grace and strength transform what looks like a problem for you into an opportunity to witness to other people. I remember what the apostle Paul wrote. *"We are afflicted in every way, but not crushed; perplexed, but not despairing; persecuted, but not forsaken; struck down, but not destroyed"* (2 Corinthians 4:8–9).

It's true that we can be discouraged, but we're never in despair. We can be knocked down by test results time and time again, but we're never knocked out. We can be surrounded by enemies on every side, but never without a friend. And the truth is, our faithful friend is none other than our Lord who promised, *"I will not leave you as orphans; I will come to you"* (John 14:18).

I was approached by two ladies at a conference in Charlotte, North Carolina a few weeks back. Both of them had lost their husbands to cancer. They had heard that I had cancer surgery, and what they shared really blessed my spirit.

They both discussed husbands who had died within two years of each other. "Our husbands' lives were a tremendous witness for the Lord," they said, "because before, during, and after their cancer, people saw no change in their spiritual make-up. The pain they suffered was obvious and, ultimately, both men died. But they were sharing Christ up until the day the Lord called them home."

In fact, one of these men led a Bible study in his Sunday school class—two days prior to his death on a Tuesday. He refused to let cancer stop him from doing what God had called him to do. Each of the women remarked, "Even to this day, we still have people come up to us and remark how much our husbands blessed their lives because they were so positive."

What great examples of committed Christians both of these men were! I have personally been touched and challenged not to let my cancer experience sway me from the ministry to which God has called me. And both of these widows, who probably were in their mid-60s, were still praising God, even though they obviously missed their husbands. Their emotional pain and loneliness did not prevent them from giving glory to God. In the balance of life, one would reasonably expect both of these widows to go home to be with the Lord within the next twenty years or so themselves, along with virtually all of their contemporaries. So what will really be important? Only what they did with their lives—not how or why they died.

GOD IS FAITHFUL

As you might expect, I could have turned this chapter into a Bible drill in which we surveyed every Scripture in God's Word dealing with the topic of suffering, but I trust that you get my drift by now. God is a *faithful* God. He is a *forgiving* God. He will forgive anything and everything on the basis of the sacrifice of His Son, the Lord Jesus Christ.

In contrast, He forgives nothing, no matter how small the event or the offense, on the basis of how good we are (or aren't), how acceptable we are, and whether our slates have more positives than negatives on them. God is *merciful.* He cares about the pain and suffering you are experiencing, whether it's physical, mental, emotional, or spiritual. Trust Him and He will give you peace—not escape—*peace.*

I think that my favorite Bible character, in regard to suffering, is King David. David suffered a lot in his life. Even before he was king, he suffered at the hands of a maniacal King Saul. Saul tried to kill him because he feared David, and he was jealous and egotistical. As a result, David ran for his life with Saul in hot pursuit all across Israel. Yet God protected David because He still had plans for his life.

But remember that David did die—as all flesh must. Bear in mind that no one—no one—can remove us one second before God decides it's our time.

God has plans that are still at work in your life. I know because you're able to read this book. God hasn't completed His work in you, so get with His program. Honor Him in the midst of your suffering. Your example may indeed have eternal consequences for those in your sphere of influence who have yet to believe in Jesus Christ.

---

1. "Murder in the Outposts: Christianity's Modern Martyrs," *Breakpoint with Chuck Colson,* April 1, 1996, No. 60401.

CHAPTER EIGHT

Thoughts from Judy Burkett

F ew things in life are as upsetting as having a loved one facing a serious or life-threatening illness and not knowing what the outcome will be. Such a situation triggers powerful, competing emotions in the lives of families and friends. On the one hand, there's a feeling of complete helplessness in the desire to take away the hurt and pain.

Even though medical treatments can help, only God can ultimately sustain a person's life here on earth. On the other hand, there's an urgent willingness to do anything and everything *within one's power* to bring comfort and hope to your loved one.

I know. I experienced those same emotions following the news of Larry's cancer. I never will forget the look on his face after he received that distressing phone call from the radiologist in Gainesville. Larry's whole demeanor had changed. I knew something was terribly wrong. As he related the story of the "mass" the MRI revealed, a tremendous wave of helplessness hit me. And I felt a loss of control.

GATHERING MY WITS

As I tried to pinpoint a Bible verse that might help me balance my feelings, I settled on Psalm 30:5: *"Weeping may last for the night, but a shout of joy comes in the morning."*

That verse not only allowed for the true fear and grief I felt then, but it also speaks of real hope for anyone who is suffering. It allows for true human emotions and for weeping; but, at the same time, it reminds us that God can and will lead us through every setback and valley we face.

In those first few days, we wavered between shock, disbelief, and thinking surely there was a mistake. Ultimately, we came to a conscious decision that we would continue to trust God in this matter, believing that He was completely in control.

It didn't occur to either of us to ask God, "Why is this happening?" Instead, as the initial shock wore off, we began to focus more on "How are we going to cope with this?" And we found that we could fight off those paralyzing feelings of helplessness by committing ourselves to the hard work of prayer.

INSIDE OUR PRAYER CLOSET: HOW WE PRAYED

When we first learned of the tumor, my first instinct was to keep it quiet and not let others know until we were sure about the diagnosis. I'm just more of a private person than Larry, and I tend to want to handle things more on my own. Larry used to be private about his personal life too, but since becoming a Christian he has become very much a people person. He wanted to let everybody know about the tumor—and for good reason. He wanted all the people who would to pray earnestly for him.

There were moments when we didn't know exactly how to pray; but, some key Scriptures helped to encourage us. They reminded us that both the Holy Spirit and the Lord Jesus Himself are interceding for us, particularly when we struggle with "saying" the right words. There were times when we didn't have words at all, but we knew we were being blessed just by being silent before the Lord.

"And in the same way the Spirit also helps our weakness; for we do not know how to pray as we should, but the Spirit Himself intercedes for us with groanings too deep for words" (Romans 8:26).

"Hence, also, He is able to save forever those who draw near to God through Him, since He always lives to make intercession for them" (Hebrews 7:25).

We also had plenty of specific requests that we set before God in prayer, including the following petitions.

"GOD, PLEASE TAKE AWAY THE CANCER"

We decided to be totally honest before the Lord with our requests. First, we obviously prayed about Larry's health. If he had cancer, we prayed for God to remove it. Of course, if God chose to supernaturally heal Larry, we would rejoice; and I believe God is completely capable of doing that.

Knowing the Bible teaches that God is no respecter of persons (Romans 2:11), we did not assume that Larry had "special status" with the Lord. Sometimes God heals people outright; at other times, though faithful, godly saints succumb to serious illnesses.

However, if the answer for Larry involved surgery, we were open to that as well. I probably was more eager for him to have the surgery than he was, because I feared that he might change his mind and not have it.

I encourage you to lay out the desires of your heart before God in prayer. Be honest with Him. Don't be afraid to tell God exactly what the desires of your heart are.

"For we do not have a high priest who cannot sympathize with our weaknesses, but one who has been tempted in all things as we are, yet without sin. Let us therefore draw near with confidence to the throne of grace, that we may receive mercy and may find grace to help in a time of need" (Hebrews 4:15–16).

"GOD, GIVE US PEACE"

We prayed steadily that God would give us His peace in the midst of the turmoil. I'm reminded of the apostle Paul's promise that *"The peace of God, which surpasses all comprehension, shall guard your hearts and your minds in Christ Jesus"* (Philippians 4:7).

Larry and I have found that promise to be true. We asked God for peace, and He granted us an inner serenity that was beyond explanation. If we had tried to rationalize peace into our minds and souls, we would have been miserable. Logic cannot produce God's benefits, and Galatians 5:22 makes it very clear that God's peace comes as a fruit of the Holy Spirit.

Don't misunderstand. I'm not saying that we prayed for peace that first night and were "sealed" in a supernatural bubble from then on. There were times when we worried and were upset. And we prayed for God's peace on many occasions, particularly when we were afraid or things seemed to be spinning out of control.

And the result seemed to be the same each time: We felt like God was literally holding us in the palm of His hand. So if you're in turmoil right now because you have a loved one facing a serious health threat, let me encourage you to diligently seek God's peace. Pray specifically for it, and ask others to pray for you.

I really can't tell you how blessed and uplifted we were by the prayers of many groups of people. The word about Larry's condition spread rapidly after the first few days, especially after he went on the air the day after discovering the second tumor. We began to hear about conferences—of all sorts—that stopped during their main sessions to intercede on Larry's behalf. Special prayer meetings were called just to pray for Larry. It was a remarkable outpouring of love and support.

We heard about many people fasting and praying, including the staff at CFC, who fasted the day Larry announced his condition on the air. Within days, cards and letters began arriving at our home and at the CFC office. It took months to read them all. They were very personal messages of concern, words of encouragement, and prayer commitments.

I can tell you personally what a powerful effect all these prayers had on Larry. There were many, many days following the surgeries when he was in tremendous, agonizing pain. And of course, with major surgeries on both sides of his body, there was no comfortable position to rest in. There were days when he was discouraged and, frankly, he was inexpressibly weary of the incessant pain.

But with so many people praying for him, Larry was uplifted. A very small selection of the messages from the cards and letters are included in this book. Once you read them, I think you'll see why they had such a powerful impact on both of us. Many people wrote as if Larry were a member of their family, and they enclosed family pictures. Some wrote directly to me, expressing their concern for how the situation was affecting me. Others wrote to the ministry, telling the employees not to be discouraged—that Larry would be back. Many children drew pictures for Larry and wrote letters to him, wishing him well. The outpouring of love and concern was precious.

Let me encourage you in this matter. If you have a good word or blessing to share with someone who is ill, or even someone who has just been a real blessing to you, take the time to drop them a note or a card and say so. Galatians 6:6 states, *"And let the one who is taught the word share all good things with him who teaches."*

Larry and I, our family, and the ministry have been richly blessed by God's people who took the time to write. But we're not the only ones who needed encouragement. So does your pastor, your Sunday school teacher, that widow or single mom, or someone in your community who has been ill.

I challenge you to "give roses" while people are alive and can still enjoy them. Although beautiful flowers help to comfort a family in bereavement, they mean nothing to the deceased. Share your blessings today while they can be appreciated.

"GOD, SHOW US THE WAY"

Another issue that seemed to bubble to the forefront of our prayers was for God to supply wisdom and guidance to us. We leaned heavily on the truth of God's Word: *"Trust in the Lord with all your heart, and do not lean on your own understanding. In all your ways acknowledge Him, and He will make your paths straight"* (Proverbs 3:5–6).

We faced many decisions without the luxury of time to think them over. Doctors had to be selected. Along with that decision came the need to choose a medical center for the surgeries. Many good friends, whose opinions we deeply respect, encouraged us to consider various medical facilities throughout the country, and we had to weigh our options—carefully but quickly.

Ultimately, Larry chose the medical facility that would be closest for all of our family—Emory University Hospital in Atlanta—and one that offered some of the finest doctors and medical care available anywhere.

We also needed wisdom to clearly discern what God was responsible for and what we were to take responsibility over. That sounds simple, but often the lines of responsibility become blurred, resulting in confusion and exhaustion. After all, it's pretty hard to fill God's shoes.

Clearly discerning the things God was responsible for helped us to identify the things we needed to relinquish to Him: the first was Larry's life. Neither I, the doctors, nor anyone else could keep Larry here on earth one second longer than God desired. That's one major issue I had to give back to the Lord. Doing so also relieved a great deal of pressure, because that meant God, and no one else, was responsible for keeping Larry alive.

I have known people who second-guessed themselves because an operation didn't turn out the way they hoped and the loved one subsequently died. They had assumed responsibility for the outcome of the surgery; therefore, they struggled under a load of guilt—as though they were personally responsible for the life of the loved one. Or they harbored anger against the doctor, as if the doctor were God.

The ultimate responsibility for life here on earth rests in the hands of God. Attempting to edge in on that responsibility will only deplete your energy and emotional stamina. You weren't cut out to take responsibility for things only God can do.

Obviously you want to make the best, most intelligent decision that you can. But at a time of crisis, the best you can do is evaluate the options that you know about. Once you and your spouse agree on a plan of action, let me encourage you to relinquish your loved one to the Lord's safekeeping and trust God for the result.

The next need was for the outcome of the surgery. Larry not only was in God's hands but in the hands of skilled surgeons too. Prior to the surgeries, however, no one knew *precisely* what the operations would reveal. Some cancer operations are textbook cases, neat as a pin. Others quickly become complicated.

Since I could not effect the outcome of the surgery, I had to commit both Larry and the doctors to the Lord for the operations. In our case we were blessed with excellent Christian surgeons.

We had to stop trying to rationalize peace and simply receive peace as a gift from the Lord. As I mentioned earlier, only God can give a gift of peace that passes all understanding.

Oh, there are plenty of mind games to play. We flirted with the possibility that this whole thing was a mistake, but there was no peace with that line of reasoning. We considered that the tumors could be benign and that this would prove to be a big hubbub over nothing. That was a little more reasonable but that didn't result in true peace either.

In short, no logic could produce the peace of God. We had to seek peace from God alone and, indeed, we both found Him faithful to us.

The Serenity Prayer of St. Francis of Assisi summarizes our need to distinguish what God is responsible for versus what we are. *"God, grant me the courage to change the things I can change, the grace to accept the things I cannot change, and the wisdom to know the difference."*

"GOD, GIVE US STRENGTH"

Coping with a medical crisis is exhausting. Sleep patterns are interrupted. Comfortable daily routines get cast aside. Watching a loved one hurt is hard work too. And believe it or not, sitting around and waiting all day, either in the hospital or doctor's office, is very tiresome.

The timing for Larry's surgeries was particularly difficult for me (although I can't imagine a good time for them). I had just had surgery myself, less than a month prior to Larry's diagnosis, and my doctors advised me to be prepared for a three- to six-month recuperation myself. But even under these circumstances, God proved Himself to be faithful again.

One of the passages that helped me remain fresh comes from Isaiah 40:28–31: *"Do you not know? Have you not heard? The Everlasting God, the Lord, the Creator of the ends of the earth does not become weary or tired. His understanding is inscrutable. He gives strength to the weary, and to him who lacks might He increases power. Though youths grow weary and tired, and vigorous young men stumble badly, yet those who wait for the Lord will gain new strength; they will mount up with wings like eagles, they will run and not get tired, they will walk and not become weary."*

It helped me just to think about an eagle soaring through the air. Her responsibility is to simply stretch out her wings; God supplies the wind to keep her afloat. In other words, if she just assumes the right position, God will supply the power to keep her aloft.

As we prayed, we assumed the posture of faith—trusting God to meet our needs and to supply what we could not supply ourselves. And true to His Word, God raised us up and enabled us to endure days that we never thought we'd see the end of.

That leads to one of the most important and challenging petitions we offered to God.

"GOD, YOUR WILL BE DONE"

Our deepest desire was that God would be glorified through the circumstances we faced. I know that's easier said than done. It's very easy to pray something like, "God, let your will be done. . . ." But praying that way helped us to keep the perspective that God works in ways we cannot see and, often, tremendous blessings spring from deep tragedies. There are plenty of Bible stories that relate that truth.

After all, Larry could have died in surgery, and that was a heavy burden on my heart. But I have seen God bring Larry through some pretty difficult times and use him as a catalyst for starting many different ministries; so I just had to trust that God's hand was continuing to work, in spite of the threats to Larry's health.

"We know that God causes all things to work together for good to those who love God, to those who are called according to His purpose" (Romans 8:28).

Surprise Blessings

You've heard the saying that doctors "practice medicine," haven't you? Well, that's an accurate statement. As skilled as doctors are, medicine is still called a practice—sometimes an educated guess. Nowhere is that more evident than when the hospital asks the patient to sign the consent form prior to surgery. Basically the form releases the hospital from all liability in the event something goes wrong during an operation. It's like the hospital telling you, "We'll do the best we can, but you're on your own."

Watching Larry sign his consent form was hard, but it underscored the truth that he was in God's hands all along. But God was faithful to us, and He sent some uplifting surprises our way from unexpected sources.

First, we were incredibly blessed by having Christian doctors and nurses ministering to us. I know unbelievers can be just as skilled, but knowing that your medical personnel are of the same faith helps to create a deep "soul-bond." And when someone you love has his or her life on the line, you want everything going for them that you can. So for those of you who serve the Lord in the medical field, it means the world to have staff who understand the concept of holistic health care that includes the dimensions of body, soul, and spirit.

Friends and family were a constant source of strength for us. As Larry told you, we were particularly blessed by having our good friend Dr. Hyde with us. Not only did he accompany Larry into surgery, but he kept us advised about the progress of the surgeries. Since doctors are understandably in a hurry, it was great to have Dr. Hyde with us to leisurely answer our questions as they arose. And his wit! Frequently the tension was broken by his dry sense of humor that kept us laughing.

When the nurses questioned Dr. Hyde's reason for being in surgery he said, "I'm here just in case the patient needs an emergency hysterectomy." (Dr. Hyde is a gynecologist.) That gave them a good laugh.

Though it may sound redundant, we really did find special encouragements from God in His Word. One of the passages that meant so much when our son Dan was in the hospital years ago continued to be a source of inspiration for me.

In part it says, *"He who dwells in the shelter of the Most High will abide in the shadow of the Almighty. I will say to the Lord, 'My refuge and my fortress, My God, in whom I trust!' For it is He who delivers you from the snare of the trapper, and from the deadly pestilence. He will cover you with His pinions, and under His wings you may seek refuge; His faithfulness is a shield and bulwark. . . . Because he has loved Me, therefore I will deliver him; I will set him securely on high, because he has known My name. He will call upon Me, and I will answer him; I will be with him in trouble; I will rescue him, and honor him. With a long life I will satisfy him, and let him behold My salvation"* (Psalm 91:1–4,14–16).

Detecting God's blessings requires an awareness that God can and does provide daily evidences of His presence. Watching for His work in your particular circumstances takes tremendous discipline, since it is easy to be overcome with emotions like fear or anger. So you need focus. Talking to your friends and family about God's blessings in the midst of your pain will lead to the following results.

1. You'll be a witness to others for Jesus Christ.

Telling others about God's provision for you will strengthen your faith. Acts 1:8 says, *"You shall be My witnesses . . . even to the remotest part of the earth."*

2. Since others may overlook the blessing you discovered, tell them.

According to John 1:45, after discovering the Messiah in Jesus Christ, Philip immediately told Nathanael about his exciting discovery. In Matthew 28:8, after meeting the resurrected Jesus, the two Marys *"ran to report it to His disciples."*

3. You'll be strengthened by verbalizing God's goodness.

This is an important strategy for fighting off depression or despair. *"For as he thinks within himself, so he is"* (Proverbs 23:7). If you bombard yourself with negative, depressing thoughts, guess what the result will be? On the other hand, if you talk to others about God's goodness, your heart will be uplifted.

4. God is honored by your faith.

"Without faith, it is impossible to please Him, for he who comes to God must believe that He is, and that He is a rewarder of those who seek Him" (Hebrews 11:6). Since that is the case, I try not to be surprised or overwhelmed when God allows situations to develop in my life that require absolute faith and trust in Him.

HOW TO SERVE WITHOUT BURNING OUT

Supporting an ill family member for an extended period of time requires balance since it requires so much "giving." In the role of a literal servant, you give time, energy, and love.

Give, give, give, give, give, give—*and you'll collapse.*

Giving of yourself, under extremely stressful conditions over a long period of time, will lead to your personal burnout if you don't have a systematic means of being replenished.

Symptoms of burnout can include loss of appetite, giving up, depression, insomnia, withdrawal, bitterness, resentment, outbursts of anger, or loss of hope. If you let yourself become depleted to this point, you no longer can be much help to your loved one. So here are some ideas for how you can take care of yourself, thus allowing you to serve your loved one without getting burned out.

1. Rest.

Bedside care is exhausting work. If you remain overnight with your loved one, seldom will you get a full night's sleep. And let's face it: A fold-down chair is not a bed; it's a fold-down chair. And I don't know about you, but when nighttime comes, there's no place like being at home in my bed. If you are fortunate enough to have extended family in the area, you might consider setting up a rotation for remaining overnight. I realize that leaving your loved one's bedside may be a big step—depending on if he or she is critically ill—but you'll be better able to help if you get your rest.

2. Maintain a healthy diet.

I know your appetite is likely to evaporate when you're under a lot of stress or if you worry. And, as I can attest to, eating under those conditions can also result in stomach cramps. But keeping a healthy diet will help you to stay fresh and to be attentive to your loved one.

In some ways, your body favorably compares to a machine, such as an automobile engine. You might be able to neglect it for a while and get away with it; but long-term neglect will result in damage to the parts. Feed your body healthy foods—and that doesn't mean living off the snack machine in the waiting room at the end of the hall!

3. Exercise.

Amazingly, *using* energy will help you to become invigorated and energized. I know how hard it is to get motivated to exercise if you're beset with emotional burdens. But you have to be disciplined and make yourself do the right thing.

Taking care of yourself is an essential component of taking care of your loved one. Ask the hospital nurses or home health aides for isometric exercises recommended by the physical therapy department, and I'm sure they'll be able to help.

4. Stay organized.

Make a list of things that are changing in your life, since changes often mean responsibilities and commitments can escape your attention and go uncovered. Do you have children that others will need to pick up? If you are staying at the hospital at the moment, how will you keep your bills current?

You will find it helpful (even critical) to ask your church family to help. A good idea is to request one person to be your logistics coordinator—similar to an administrative assistant—who will coordinate daily activities. That way, if you can think of something that needs to be done, you will have someone to relay that information and get it off your mind.

5. Read and learn about your loved one's illness.

This not only will keep your mind fresh, but you may have the opportunity to share what you're learning with other families. Ask if your hospital has a small library, reading room, or chapel. Ask what resources are available through your local library. Ask your doctor to recommend books. The more you can learn about your loved one's illness, the more you can help.

My daughter Kim is very good on computers, and she was able to locate a great deal of helpful information on the Internet. If you don't have a family member who can do this, ask your pastor. Very likely he will know of someone who can help.

That's an important step, since being in the dark is frequently a breeding ground for fear. Your doctor or hospital officials can probably help you locate a support group related to your loved one's illness. Some may meet right there in the hospital.

6. Keep a journal.

I kept a personal journal during Larry's ordeal, and I can't begin to tell you what a blessing it has been. Often my thoughts clarified only as I began writing them down, and that was a big step toward clear thinking. But keeping a journal also has long-term benefits. Now, more than a year after Larry's surgeries, I can review my notes from a new perspective, and I can see even more clearly how God was with us all along.

Write your thoughts and impressions. You may not be highly motivated at the moment, but in the years ahead your reflections will be your treasure.

7. Plan to be there.

After one of the surgeries, Larry and I were both awake in the middle of the night, so we decided to take a walk down the hall together. As we walked, we softly reflected on what all this ordeal was about. As we neared the room again, he said to me, "You pinch me and I'll pinch you, and maybe we'll wake up from this nightmare."

There were many, many intimate times of sharing together, just like that one, for Larry and me because I was committed to being with him. We survived the ups and downs together.

But more than just time with one another, there are other benefits of remaining at the hospital as much as possible. For one thing, you can remain up-to-date on your loved one's progress by talking with the doctors and nurses during visits. Ask questions. Learn what medications are being administered and the anticipated effect they will have. Often you can provide important details or observations to the staff that the patient can't—or sometimes won't.

Being at the hospital also helps the nursing staff. With all the hullabaloo over medical costs, most hospitals have downsized the number of nurses on their shifts, which means that patients may have to wait for personal attention. If you are there, you can assist with getting a drink, adjusting pillows, feeding a meal, helping to the rest room, or just fussing with the third shift nurses who very often are too overworked to check their patients in a timely fashion.

8. Talk to your pastor or the hospital chaplain.

These religious professionals offer objectivity, hope, and a stabilizing element to your situation. The hospital chaplain, in particular, is often willing to serve as an intermediary with the hospital staff about recurring problems you may be facing. They also can provide important insights into the hospital administration, such as who to talk to about your insurance, hospital bills, or procedures within the hospital.

Since most chaplains are on call twenty-four hours a day, don't hesitate to have them pray with you and your loved one, especially if you reach a point of being exhausted, your hope is diminished, or if your loved one's health takes a turn for the worse.

If you're at home, of course your pastor or church leaders represent an important connection to your church family. If he is not a stranger to your home, he'll have personal insights and encouragements that flow from his heart. However, if you're presently without a church family or pastor, now is a great time to establish a relationship. I know it will feel awkward, but let me encourage you to call a pastor in your town, explain your situation, and request a visit. Most churches and pastors would be elated to establish contacts with families in need. They really would count it a privilege and joy to serve you.

9. Maintain your spiritual disciplines of Bible study and prayer.

It's really easy to let your Bible study slide when your routines get disrupted and you're distracted by critical illness in your family. But God's Word is powerful.

First Thessalonians 2:13 says that *"[God's Word] performs its work in you who believe."* Hebrews 4:12 describes God's Word as *"living and active."* It will gently refresh you with God's constant presence and provision in your life. It will bring balance and perspective to your thoughts by subduing panic and fear. Just as your physical body needs nourishment, so does your personal faith.

10. Find a way to treat yourself.

Walk outside. Connect with other families in the hospital. If you like to read, get a good book (like this one) and read it. You may splurge a dollar or two at the candy machine, or bring a twelve-pack of your favorite carbonated drink to the room. Or how about *fresh donuts* during the midnight watch?

What you do is not as important as finding something that represents mental relief, relaxation, and refreshment for you. Little doses of personal attention to yourself will help to regain perspective, especially if your caring has become a twenty-four-hour-a-day job.

11. Cultivate your sense of humor.

"A joyful heart is good medicine, but a broken spirit dries up the bones" (Proverbs 17:22). Following one of his surgeries, Larry apparently had a reaction to one of the narcotic painkillers, because he woke up in the middle of the night, sat up on the side of the bed, and said, "Judy, let's go. I'm going for a drive."

I had been snoozing on the fold-down recliner chair in the corner, but I quickly roused to attention and assured him, "Larry you're not going to drive anywhere. You're in the hospital."

"No, I'm not," he said. "I'm getting out of here. I'm going for a drive."

Thinking he was faking, I said, "Well, I'll just have to go get the nurse."

"I don't care if you get the nurse or not. I'm leaving this place," Larry insisted.

Of course he wasn't able to go anywhere, and the nurse got him settled back down, but the family had a good laugh about his determination to "go for a drive."

Sometimes you have to laugh to keep from crying. Because a serious illness often triggers reunions of family members and friends, a good source of humor is simply reflecting on old times together.

One word of caution: Be aware that each person may not be "in the mood" for levity at the same time. A hysterical moment to some may occur precisely in a moment of despair for another family member, leaving that person thinking, "How can they be cutting up at a time like this?"

The best plan is to be open with one another and respectful of the feelings of others. That may mean moving "the party" to the lobby of the hospital or to another, more remote room in the house.

I conclude with this thought: *God made you.* He knows what you can and cannot handle. He promises never to give you a burden you cannot bear without a way of escape. When you find yourself overwhelmed and exhausted by the stress of it all, you may well be taking on more than God wants you to assume. Remember, you're just a *part* of God's plan.

CHAPTER NINE

The Search for an Alternative Treatment

But Larry, these alternative treatments are untested and unreliable. We don't know what risks they present," said a friend in his attempt to counter my arguments. "There are no hard statistics on how effective these alternative treatments are." I had been trying to convince my friend, a congressman, of the need for the FDA (Food and Drug Administration) to loosen the tight restrictions on testing new cancer drugs and treatments in the United States.

"Okay, how about this?" I asked. "One treatment I heard about is toxic to the human body. Doctors typically purchase it for $50 per dose and sell it for $2,000 per dose to the patient, and many patients who take this treatment do not survive more than five years. Would you allow doctors to continue treatment like that?," I asked.

After pausing to think, the congressman answered, "No way. That doesn't sound very effective to me."

"That's precisely my point," I responded. "I just described what many patients on chemotherapy are facing. The FDA is applying a more stringent standard to new treatments than they have to traditional chemotherapy."

Somehow, there has to be a better way to treat cancer than chemotherapy and radiation, without all the negative side effects. And until we can find it, it seems logical to me that we as Americans should be able to choose a treatment of choice, especially if it can be proved that the treatment is not inherently harmful to the human body.

It is expected that 555,000 Americans will die in 1996 from cancer. That's about 215,000 more than in 1971 when President Richard Nixon declared a war on the disease. The National Cancer Institute spent about $29 billion on cancer research in the last quarter of a century.[1]

Progress has been made in some cancer recoveries. For instance, from 1973 to 1991, the death rate from colon and rectal cancer has dropped 15 percent. During those same years, however, deaths from lung cancer have soared 42 percent. In spite of our best efforts, it would seem that we should be making more progress in the treatment of cancer.

Many doctors point out that in the United States we still employ the same basic treatments that were available twenty-five years ago, namely, chemotherapy and radiation. Based on the number of people I've personally known who didn't survive these debilitating therapies, I have to ask myself, "Is this the best we can do? Are the current cancer treatments good enough in light of these staggering numbers?"

Obviously medical experts are looking for better treatments, but the complex rules established by the FDA leave only the largest companies with the resources to get new therapies approved. I suspect that all too often the incentive to develop cheaper, less toxic treatments conflicts with the return needed on previous drugs.

Discussing the effectiveness of cancer treatments here in the United States is a very complex matter. And let me assure you that I am not presenting myself as a medical expert, either in terms of traditional or alternative therapies. I do, however, have a personal testimony to share. As I alluded to earlier in the book, I want to be a faithful steward of all that God has entrusted to me, including my cancer experiences—both good and bad.

One of the reasons choosing a cancer treatment is so complex is that there are quite a number of variables to consider. Consider the following.

- There is a variety of chemotherapy drugs available.
- Particular cancers respond differently to this variety of drugs.
- Each person's body is unique and may very well respond to drugs differently than another patient. Thus, what works for one patient may not work as well for another.
- Both chemotherapy and radiation have side effects, but those symptoms may vary widely from person to person.

So you can quickly see that the co-mingling of these variables makes traditional cancer therapies very complex to describe and often very confusing to the patient. As a result, it is not uncommon for the patient to simply leave the responsibility for a decision totally in the hands of the doctor. But doctors have limits on knowledge also, and it is *your* body they're treating. *You must take the initiative to become informed and take responsibility for your treatment.*

To help clarify the discussion of traditional cancer therapies and their potential effects on you, study the following analogy.

WAR WITHIN YOUR BODY

Your battle against cancer compares favorably to a literal war inside your body. To be more precise, it's an internal revolution, and it will make a difference in your treatment and in your recovery. Cancer cells are fighting to conquer your body, and if they win, your life here on earth will be over.

These cancer cells are the enemy forces and the friendly forces are your immune system. Other factors to consider in this internal battle are the terrain (where the cancer is located), the enemy's degree of entrenchment (how long the cancer has been there), the readiness of your troops for battle (how strong your immune system is), and attack strategies (specific plans to neutralize and eradicate the cancer). Your task, along with the doctors you hire, is to identify and beat back the cancer cells that will multiply and overcome your body unless they are stopped.

Identifying the Enemy

To win the battle, you have to accurately identify who the enemy is—and the sooner the better. In the Vietnam conflict of the 1960s and early 1970s, one of the challenges for American troops was simply distinguishing the Viet Cong troops from civilians.

In the battle against cancer, you and your doctors must identify what the cancer is. For this reason I would encourage you to avail yourself of the diagnostic tests necessary to determine if you have cancer and, if so, precisely what kind you have. Remember, there are competent doctors in oncology, just like in any other field, and there are incompetent doctors. You really want to seek out the former.

An article in *USA Today* underscores the importance of selecting your doctor carefully.

- "License revocations, suspensions and other actions rose 58% from 1991 to 1995, according to unpublished data from the federally mandated National Practitioner Data Bank.

- The number of physicians facing disciplinary action each year rose 47% during the same period, according to the Federation of State Medical Boards.

- And the number of names in 'Questionable Doctors,' a compendium maintained by the consumer group Public Citizen, has grown 89% to 13,012 since 1990."[2]

I have found the best way to learn about a doctor's reputation is simply by referral. Call one of the local support groups in your community and ask for referrals for the best doctors that regularly deal with your type of cancer (or any other disease). Remember, it's your body and you are paying a doctor (or doctors) to help you take care of it.

You may have the temptation to "look the other way" and ignore the symptoms of irregularities in your health. Let me tell you: *Ignorance is not bliss; instead, it could be fatal.* At the first hint that your body is experiencing irregularities, set an appointment with your doctor to discover what's going on. What is only a minor problem today can become life threatening if it is neglected.

Study the following table to become acquainted with the most common and lethal kinds of cancer known in America today, along with their projected five-year survival rates.

The Most Deadly Cancers[3]	
TYPE OF CANCER	**FIVE-YEAR SURVIVAL RATE FOR TRADITIONAL THERAPIES**
1. Lung	13 percent
2. Colorectal	diagnosed early, 91 percent; when cancer has spread to surrounding organs or lymph nodes, 63 percent; when cancer has spread to distant organs, less than 7 percent
3. Breast	for localized tumors, 96 percent; when cancer has spread to lymph nodes, 75 percent; when cancer has spread to other parts of the body, 20 percent
4. Prostate	85 percent
5. Pancreatic	4 percent
6. Lymphoma	for Hodgkin's disease, 80 percent; for non-Hodgkin's lymphoma, 51 percent
7. Leukemia	38 percent average; however, acute myelocytic leukemia is only 10 percent; acute lymphocytic leukemia is higher at 52 percent
8. Liver	6 percent
9. Ovarian	44 percent; if the cancer has not spread, 91 percent
10. Stomach	8 percent
11. Brain	25 percent
12. Kidney	58 percent
13. Bladder	before spreading, 93 percent; spread to nearby tissue, 49 percent; spread to distant organs, 6 percent
14. Esophageal	3 percent to 6 percent

Friendly Forces

Your immune system is your primary ally to do battle against the forces of cancer. The stronger your immune system, the better job you can do in battling the cancer. Your immune system can be strengthened through good nutrition and specialized therapies. The Bible says that your body is a temple of the Holy Spirit (1 Corinthians 6:19–20) and that you are to glorify God with your body. You can actually cooperate with and build up your immune system through maintaining a healthy diet, getting plenty of sleep at night, regular exercise, and taking steps to minimize stress in your life.

The Terrain

Just exactly where is the enemy (the cancer) located? In traditional warfare, terrain plays a critical role in developing an attack strategy. Think back to Germany's invasion of Russia in World War II and the role that the frigid winter snows played in halting Germany's progress. More recently, in the Gulf War of the early 1990s, Middle East sands were a critical factor that had to be taken into account as the Allied forces drove the Iraqis from Kuwait.

The location of the cancer plays a major factor in developing your battle strategy. A cancer encapsulated in a single tumor will likely be easier to battle than cancer that has metastasized (spread) to other parts of your body. *One* battle front is easier to defend than multiple battle fronts. In my particular situation, our concern was heightened when we learned that the cancer in my shoulder was a secondary tumor—meaning that it had metastasized from somewhere else in my body.

In warfare, a host of modern technologies can help to pinpoint the enemy's location and movements, including satellite photographs, surveillance flights, and radar. In the battle against cancer, CAT scans, MRIs, and many newly developed diagnostic tests help to locate the cancer. Take advantage of these services to discover precisely what's happening in your body.

The Enemy's Degree of Entrenchment

Along with the enemy's location, a knowledge of *how long* the enemy has been organizing for battle is a must. Obviously, the less time the enemy has had to set up operations, the better for you. The more entrenched the enemy has become, generally the more difficult it is to root it out. You may recall how difficult and bloody the battle of Iwo Jima was in World War II, precisely because the Japanese troops were so deeply entrenched in the island's caves and rocks.

For that reason, it is very important that you investigate abnormalities or significant changes in your bodily functions. In nearly all cancer therapies, early detection is a major factor in winning the battle against cancer. If you suspect something's not quite right, getting yourself checked out is a "win-win" situation, although you cannot rely on just one or two "opinions."

You need to understand your own body and have confidence in your own diagnostic abilities, as well as those of your doctors! I am a walking example that doctors, even good doctors, can be wrong. I had at least two orthopedic specialists assure me that the pain I felt in my shoulder was bursitis and should be treated with steroids. Had I accepted that analysis, most likely I would be another cancer statistic today.

If there's no problem, you can dismiss your concerns from your mind. If you indeed have a problem with cancer, you've taken steps to catch it early. My encouragement is for you to avail yourself of medical care quickly if you think you are experiencing any unusual health symptoms.

CURRENT ATTACK STRATEGIES

American medical science typically pursues one or more of the three treatments for cancer: surgery, chemotherapy, radiation. But even as sophisticated as American medical science is, these cancer treatments amount to cutting, poisoning, or burning, to put it bluntly. After briefly discussing these three, I want to detail for you what attracted me to alternative cancer therapies.

Surgery

This is obviously the choice I made as the first step in battling my cancer. My thinking was to get the cancer out of my body if possible. That's similar to America's objective in the Gulf War: remedy the situation by simply evicting the Iraqis from Kuwait.

Unfortunately, not all cancers are operable. Those that involve vital organs like the liver, heart, lungs, and pancreas are particularly aggressive and difficult to excise surgically.

I personally have nothing but praise for the physicians and staff who treated me. They were skilled, caring professionals, as are most health care workers today, but in the final analysis the decisions were mine and Judy's, and I wanted all the counsel I could get. Ultimately, I elected to have surgery as the first step in my battle plan.

Chemotherapy

Chemotherapy is a variety of poisons used to attack and destroy cancer cells. Unfortunately, they do not always distinguish between good, healthy cells and the cancer cells. So, in the crudest sense, the strategy of using chemotherapy is one of introducing poison into your body and hoping the good cells outlast the bad cells. In comparison to the Gulf War, this would have amounted to America using chemical warfare on the front lines of the battle in order to kill the enemy. The problem is that the chemicals can potentially kill your own troops, and you just have to hope you have more reinforcements than the enemy. If the enemy holds out longer, you have lost.

Chemotherapy is a potent caustic agent. I personally know a nurse who had a syringe explode, spewing the substance all over her face and arms. She partially lost the sight in her left eye, and the skin on her face, hands, and chest peeled off as a result. It is only because God created our veins with such a resilient construction that our bodies can survive even a dose of this poison. But often, it is at a high cost to our immune systems and vital organs.

Indeed, in some cases chemotherapy can only inhibit the growth of the cancer but not eradicate it. As you might imagine, a person's immune system (your battle troops) can become substantially run down during a series of chemotherapy treatments. As a result, the patient's body can become susceptible to other infections or illnesses that actually overcome the person—rather than the cancer.

I was saddened to hear of the death of Michelle Carew, daughter of baseball-great Rod Carew, in the spring of 1996. Michelle, only eighteen years old, had suffered from leukemia. The headlines of the Thursday, April 18, 1996 issue of *USA Today*'s sports section read, "Michelle Carew, 18, dies of leukemia."[4] But the article went on to say that she really died from complications as a result of the chemotherapy. She died of cardiac and respiratory failure. Although she might have eventually died from the leukemia, it was *the treatment*—chemotherapy—that ultimately took her life.

Erma Bombeck, the witty satirist who made the plight of the average housewife into a never-ending string of funny stories, died in April of 1996 from what was reported as renal (kidney) failure as a result of chemotherapy, used to combat her breast cancer.

Chemotherapy can have some very debilitating effects, including the loss of hair, nausea, weight loss, anemia, and major organ failure. Those should all be considered before choosing this treatment.

Radiation

This therapy pinpoints high-level dosages of radiation in powerful beams to the location of the cancer in your body. The goal is to either kill the cancer cells or at least thwart their growth substantially. Unfortunately, the high dosage of radiation kills many other cells in the targeted areas, including some healthy and growing cells. Although that may be an acceptable risk, if you have a self-contained tumor in an extremity, such as an arm or leg, this becomes more complex if the treatment takes place in the central body cavity. Radiation also can be administered through the insertion of implants into the body in the location of the cancer.

If we compared this therapy to warfare tactics, radiation would be similar to massive bombing on the front lines of the battle. Both the "good guys" and the "bad guys" are annihilated, and the team with the most reinforcements wins. Numerous side effects, similar to chemotherapy, may also accompany the use of radiation therapy.

After surgery, I didn't have to choose between radiation or chemotherapy, since my doctors candidly told me that chemo wouldn't help and radiation wasn't called for. So the thing I asked the Lord was, "What next?"

During my recuperation I received from listeners hundreds of articles, books, audiotapes, and videotapes, describing alternative cancer treatments. Some had apparent merit; some didn't. As a result, we were able to compile in a matter of weeks what others might have taken five years to discover. My daughter Kim began sorting this information, much of which was confusing. The suggestions ranged all the way from chicken bones and magic pyramids to some rather sophisticated alternatives used by medical practitioners in other countries.

THE THREE CRITERIA FOR ALTERNATIVE THERAPIES

To evaluate all of the options, I narrowed my search for an alternative treatment by establishing three criteria.

Scientific Merit

I determined that the treatment I chose to use had to have some scientific merit. It couldn't consist of chicken bones, chants, or magic potions. When examined, the information had to have some scientific proof, based on repeatable, verifiable data. Many alternative treatments admonish participants that they must have "blind faith"—not in God but in the treatment itself. *Well,* I thought, *when you're dealing with a terminal illness like cancer, your faith in any therapy, alternative or not, might get you killed. By the time you discover the treatment isn't working, it may be too late!*

This very thing happened to a good friend of mine, when she chose to begin an alternative cancer treatment from a post office box in Wyoming. The individual providing the treatment told her that she had to have faith in it. The worse she got, the more she was admonished to "have faith" in the treatment.

Ultimately she died. There were other therapies she could have received that had more solid scientific research behind them, but she never had the opportunity. By the way, the same principle applies to traditional therapies. Know what the doctors are doing, be certain that you know the risks, and ask for previous patients' results data.

No Harm

The treatment I chose should pose no further harm to my body. In other words, it had to be nontoxic. It's bad enough to deal with the side effects of a toxic treatment, such as chemotherapy or radiation, but with those traditional approaches at least you have access to care by professional physicians who can sometimes minimize or at least monitor your reactions to the toxicity.

That's not the case with most alternative treatments. Generally you can only get these treatments "underground," and often you're going to be dealing with people who are not thoroughly trained in medicine. Therefore that means you're on your own. For that reason, any treatment I would consider must not do any further harm to my body.

Referrals

I insisted on talking to people who had taken the treatment and survived. From a scientific viewpoint, that's called anecdotal or testimonial data. The treatment offered in Prague, Czech Republic, caught my attention for three reasons. According to the testimonies of the participants we talked to, the treatment did not hurt them; it helped the vast majority of them and it cured a percentage of them, leading me to believe that it would be effective for me.

Keep in mind, many of the patients who went to Prague did so only after traditional medicine had given up hope on them and, indeed, they were suffering from some advanced stage of cancer. Often their bodies had been severely damaged by the traditional choices of chemotherapy or radiation. Even so, their survival rate was high enough to attract my attention.

NUTRITION: A GOOD FOUNDATION
FOR ALTERNATIVE THERAPIES

As I began to narrow the pool of choices, the same key component seemed to surface in each one: proper nutrition. I encourage you to learn more about the food you eat and how good nutrition can help to strengthen your immune system. The way you fuel your body is, in large part, the way your body's going to respond to diseases—whether they are cancer, colds, or the flu. The healthier your body is, the better it responds. Much of the food we eat today is no longer nutritional because the live enzymes (nutritional elements of food) have been removed, either as a part of the cooking or in the preservation process.

The nutritional value of the food you eat may not always be readily apparent. You could be eating healthy looking meals, laying off the high fatty foods, and yet not be getting enough nutritional elements like vitamins, minerals, and live enzymes. The result is that you *think* you're eating great meals when, in fact, your body is running down all the time because it's not being fed essential nutrients.

As I began to study nutrition, I found two extremes. On the one hand, Americans eat a lot of junk food. I was just as guilty as anyone else. Everyone seems to have a similar story: "I'm in a hurry." "I've got too much to do in too little time." We don't take time to eat well. Instead, we rush through the drive-through at a local fast-food restaurant and choke down a meal on the run. The truth is that most fast-foods are loaded with fat and preservatives and, eaten over a long period of time, will potentially lead to high cholesterol, heart problems, or other diseases.

The other extreme is found in many of the health food clinics around the United States, where basically people are fed a steady diet of what I consider unpalatable "health food." Granted, you're going to get good nutrition through these programs and cut down on the fat in your diet, but I questioned if I could live like that for the rest of my life.

I began looking for a good mix between a heart diet and a cancer diet, one that I could realistically stay on the rest of my life. As long as I'm alive and able, I plan to be involved in some aspect of Christian ministry, traveling around the country. So I simply cannot pack a "doggie bag" with carrots and celery sticks to eat everywhere I go.

Nor can I, as I found out, take sixty to eighty vitamin pills every day. Kim came up with a variety of things that would supplement my diet. Generally speaking, they were all good, in and of themselves. I was on shark cartilage, kelp, blue-green algae, and some awful green stuff that I had to swallow three or four times a day, *in addition to* sixty pills comprised of vitamins, minerals, and enzymes of all sorts. I didn't even know what it all was. I was literally taking fistfuls of pills! I took about three weeks of this and concluded, *I just can't do this anymore! I can't even swallow that many pills every day.*

There's a caution to keep in mind when using vitamin supplements. Too much concentration of a particular vitamin or mineral in your system can be just as dangerous as not enough. In addition, an overabundance of these elements can conflict with your system, leaving you ill. In particular, some herbs are very potent. The key is establishing nutritional balance in your system, and you may want to seek the advice of a trained nutritionist to help you arrive at the balance that's just right for you.

My need was to stay practical. I had no intention of carrying a juicer everywhere to juice apples, oranges, carrots, persimmons, and broccoli. Can you imagine trying to haul all that through an airport?

MY PLAN OF ATTACK
Achieve Nutritional Balance in My Diet

Although I desired to achieve nutritional balance in my diet, I realized I didn't know where I was out of balance. So I began my action plan with a blood test, designed to reveal my vitamin, mineral, and enzyme levels, as well as any heavy metals in my system like mercury or lead. Any good doctor who specializes in nutritional therapy can order these tests.

The reports indicated that my overall nutritional balance was pretty good, but a few deficiencies became apparent. My level of zinc, magnesium, aluminum, and vitamins A and B were out of balance; my beta carotene was low; and a few of my enzymes were also low. Armed with that information, I looked for a product that would give me a balanced diet without having to swallow a mountain of pills, sawdust, and kelp every day. Barley green or other dark green vegetable extracts turned out to be a good supplement for the minerals. It took a long time to get used to the "strange" taste.

I eventually settled on a supplement composed exclusively of dehydrated fruits and vegetables in which the bulk, salt, and unhelpful ingredients have been removed through a flash-drying or freeze-drying process. Then the residue is further condensed into the form of a pill containing all the basic minerals and vitamins you need, but none of it is artificial. There are many good supplements available, either through good health food stores or home delivery plans.

With most hectic schedules like mine, some daily supplements are essential. But who among us has time (or stomach space) to eat all of the raw fruits and vegetables we need every day? I don't, but I can swallow a few capsules each day. Let me make it clear that I'm not laying out any nutritional plan for you. What works for me might not be helpful to you at all. My point is simply to share the truth of what I have experienced. In my case, it seemed reasonable to use a good supplement and to do so every day—in addition to eating a good, balanced diet.

I subsequently checked my vitamin, mineral, and enzyme levels and all my levels were restored to normal again. My beta carotene level was high and that was particularly good news, since I have read that beta carotene helps your body to fight off the free radicals that are thought to contribute to cancer. Nonetheless, I would caution that you still have to take responsibility for making your own medical decisions, including nutrition.

Eventually I chose the treatment in Prague because it looked best for me. I have tried at least two other therapies that met my personal criteria for treatment. What works for one person does not necessarily work for everyone else. There are two real keys to finding what is best for you and your loved ones: get educated (read, listen, watch, and ask) and keep a positive attitude (a negative, defeated attitude will kill you).

Stop Drinking Tap Water

I have determined to stop drinking tap water for a couple of reasons. First, now that I only have one kidney, the last thing I want is a kidney stone. In an effort to help my kidney all I can, I have settled on drinking filtered, ozonated water. That's a general rule. If I'm eating out, I feel free to drink small amounts of tap water, but when I have a choice I try to stick to bottled water.

I should add that I supplement that with drinking juices with plenty of minerals because they replenish my electrolytes, which may be depleted by a steady diet of bottled water. From what I understand, low levels of electrolytes can lead to some kind of arrhythmia of the heart, and I don't need to stir up heart problems. Again, this is just my personal testimony of what's working for me.

Read Everything I Can Find on My Kind of Cancer

Until I was diagnosed with cancer, I actually knew very little about it or even the immune system that God created in our bodies. I just didn't have the need to know much about it. The Burkett family has no history of cancer, though most suffered from heart ailments. But the discovery of the two tumors changed all that. I became an avid student of cancer, reading anything and everything I could get my hands on. As I outlined at the beginning of the chapter, I needed to understand the war being waged in my body. In particular, I was interested in discovering the most effective treatments around for renal cell carcinoma.

I say this because I have met lots of people who with the discovery of cancer turn their heads the other way and choose to remain uninformed about it. Some suppose that if they learn about the cancer that knowledge will somehow unleash its destructive effects in their bodies.

Just think about that. What you understand in your brain *can't accelerate* the spread of cancer. To the contrary, the faster you face the battle being waged within, the more opportunity you have to help your body counter the disease. Just don't allow yourself to dwell on it.

Remember back in the summer of 1990 when Iraq invaded Kuwait? How much good did it do for Kuwait to ignore the buildup of Saddam Hussein's armies on its own northern borders? None! Ignoring the threat of invasion only made it easier for the Iraqis to proceed with their invasion.

Let me encourage you to read everything you can about the illness you're battling against. Discover how you can help your body's immune system do what God created it to do. Especially in the case of cancer, early detection and swift action are two key steps to surviving the assault on your body.

The Alternative Treatment in Prague

Several factors attracted my attention to an alternative cancer treatment provided in Prague, Czech Republic, and the more I learned, the more convinced I became to try it.

You'll remember, I told you that leaders from my church came to pray over me prior to my surgeries and that, when the others left, Dr. Bill White remained behind. Bill was the first to tell me about the treatments in Prague, and he knew of a cancer patient who had gone there. The patient proved to be a mutual acquaintance with an interesting testimony.

After being diagnosed with melanoma, this man, whom I'll call Jim, was told that he only had a few weeks to live—a few months at most (which, by the way, is wrong for any doctor to say since no one has the ability to predict such things with any degree of accuracy). After taking the treatment in Prague, however, Jim is still very much alive and, after a year and a half, he's doing quite well. To my knowledge, his cancer wasn't cured, but it's either in remission or has drastically slowed down, which gives him time to search out other therapies.

Based on Jim's story, my interest in the Prague treatment was sparked. The question was, did the treatment meet my three criteria: *Did it have scientific merit? Were there survivors of the treatment? Would the treatment pose further harm to my body?*

The formula (drug) offered in Prague actually was developed by a doctor in Greece who used it to treat ulcers (a common malady in Greece). According to newspaper reports of the time, many of his patients with cancer discovered that their cancer either disappeared or had gone into remission. As a result, he began to treat terminally ill patients—in particular, patients whom traditional medicine had given up on. Sure enough, between 30 and 40 percent (his estimate) recovered. He believed he had a significant find.

When the Communists fell from power in 1989, one of the doctor's colleagues talked him into moving his clinic from Athens, Greece to Prague, because of the renowned biochemists in the Czech Republic. While under Soviet domination, the Russians paid premium salaries to Czech biochemists to develop germ warfare weapons. On average, they made up to $60 a month, compared to $10 a month for a typical doctor. The brightest Czech minds, of course, gravitated toward the field of biochemistry, which resulted in a ready supply of qualified scientists available, once the Communists withdrew.

I called the clinic in Prague to obtain more specific information and talked to the director, who was born in Czechoslovakia and did her university studies here in the United States, where she married an American citizen. (The address for the clinic is in the Appendix.) I learned the following about the treatment.

- Although the formula had a long record of helping people with cancer (according to the inventor), formal research notes had not been kept by the doctor in Greece.
- Clinical studies were presently being conducted, using mice, and the preliminary results were very positive.
- While the clinic director wouldn't promise that the formula would help me, she was convinced that it clearly helped to boost the entire immune system, which would aid in the treatment of cancer.

Although the research on this treatment was less than complete, I was satisfied by knowing that some of the world's finest biochemists were conducting clinical studies on this treatment; and there was a reasonable scientific approach to it.

Another criterion for selecting a cancer treatment was equally important: There had to be survivors with whom I could talk. In other words, it had to have some measurable degree of success. The clinic was happy to provide names of people we could talk to, and Kim and I contacted about twenty-five.

Of that number several had died, in which case we asked their loved ones what they thought about the treatment. Without exception each highly recommended it. They said that their loved one's pain was significantly reduced due to the treatment, they lived longer, and they had a better quality of life than expected. Keep in mind, many of these people sought out the alternative treatment in Prague *only* after traditional medicine had given up on them. Most suffered from very advanced stages of cancer, and more often than not chemotherapy or radiation had significantly damaged body organs and their immune systems.

It's true that the Czechs do not have the best medical facilities around. I've seen some of their hospitals, which are very clean, but they're also very spartan. They lack materials and medical supplies, and they work with some pretty ancient instruments and machines (former socialism at its best). No one in the world can match the facilities in the United States in those areas. The Czechs have a high caliber of chemistry, and the Prague laboratory matches any in the world. While we were in Prague we met many others who had obviously benefitted from the treatment and were returning for follow-up work.

The criterion I set for prospective cancer treatments, that of posing no further harm to my body, was also met by the Prague treatment. They revealed the basic ingredients of the formula and my doctor verified that a compound made up of these ingredients would pose no threat to my health. There was nothing in it that was toxic to the human body. In addition, the cost was quite reasonable (about $2,000 at that time, plus travel and lodging).

Quite unlike traditional chemotherapy, the net effect of this formula is to drastically boost the immune system in order to counteract the attacks of the cancer. Using the analogy of warfare, this amounts to supplying more and more troops and sophisticated weapons to the front lines, rather than bombing the front lines with chemical weapons (chemotherapy) that kill everything in sight.

The treatment in Prague was very simple. I received twenty injections over a twenty-four day period. After that initial treatment, I have to take booster shots about once every six months. That's all. And the entire trip, including treatment, airfare, lodging, and meals for two costs about the same as one day in the hospital here in the U.S.! The only difference is that insurance will pay for the hospital care but not for the alternative treatment.

I'm not in a position to make claims and promises for anyone else regarding this treatment. What I can tell you is that six other people who were diagnosed with renal cell carcinoma at about the same time I was have all died within the last year. I'm still alive, I feel good, and I'm not suffering from cancer at this point. Individual circumstances? Perhaps. The prayers of God's people? Absolutely!

I'm still in pain daily from the surgeries, but hopefully that will diminish with time. God is not finished working through my life as yet, and He has graciously spared me. And I know that somehow, even though I don't totally know how, God has used this alternative cancer therapy from Prague as part of my answer to prayer. The certainty is that He has given me a real peace about it.

IT'S TIME TO REFORM THE FDA

I personally think it's ridiculous that this treatment and others like it are not available to patients here in the United States. The treatment is not legal because it can't pass the stringent requirements passed by the FDA (Food and Drug Administration). I might add, incidently, that the many chemotherapy drugs, vastly more toxic and harmful to the human body than the majority of these alternative treatments, are legal and available but probably wouldn't pass the current screening system.

In my judgment, if a particular treatment can be proved to be nontoxic, and it has a reasonably verifiable track record of helping people, the FDA should get out of the way and let American citizens make their own decisions about what treatment to pursue. This is a free country, and we're supposed to be free people.

Even if a particular treatment doesn't cure cancer, I should still have the right to make my own choice. What upsets me is that there are existing treatments that *can* help people but the system won't even allow doctors to mention them.

I am concerned that the current system exists to protect some large and politically influential financial interests, rather than to serve hurting people who are desperate for help. I know there are literally thousands of cancer patients around the country who are dying because they either can't tolerate the traditional medicines—chemotherapy or radiation—or because they don't work for them. There is no excuse for such limitations on medical options for people living in a free country.

Is there a risk associated with alternative therapies? Of course. There's a calculated risk regardless of the treatment you choose, even if you choose no treatment at all. But if you're a terminal patient dying with cancer, you've got a 100 percent risk of dying if you do nothing. So the way I see it is, if all normal options are exhausted, any risk you take can only improve your opportunity to live longer, with a better quality of life. If the price is reasonable and the patient agrees, I say, "Go for it."

---

1. "The War on Cancer," *U.S. News and World Report,* February 1996, p.54.
2. "Patients Deserve to Know Details About Their Docs," *USA Today,* May 22, 1996.
3. "The Most Deadly Cancers," *U.S. News and World Report,* February 5, 1996, pp. 62–67.
4. "Michelle Carew, 18, dies of leukemia," *USA Today,* April 18, 1996.

CHAPTER TEN

◆

Physicians' Perspectives on Alternative Treatments

NO NEWS IS BAD NEWS

*I*t's hard to describe the new trends in conventional medicine when it comes to new cancer therapies, because it appears to me, as a layman, that there really aren't any. The old adage goes, "No news is good news," but in this case the opposite is true. No news in the battle against cancer is not good. As I said earlier, the most common conventional treatments—surgery, chemotherapy, and radiation—have all been in use for the past thirty or forty years. They are not new. Yet, more people than ever are dying from cancer, even after billions and billions of dollars have been spent on research over decades.

After watching family, friends, and neighbors die agonizing deaths, there's a groundswell of people beginning to say, "If I get cancer, I'm willing to try something—anything—new." And with good reason. Many of the newer chemotherapeutic drugs are proving to be more toxic to the human body, yet not a bit more effective, in terms of arresting the spread of cancer. So how can we win the battle against cancer *with medicines that often destroy the body?*

We've got access to the best medical research laboratories in the world; billions upon billions of dollars have been spent to finance the research; the United States has thousands of physicians who genuinely do care about people. So why the stalemate?

To help shed light on the lack of progress, as well as to help you understand how conventional and alternative cancer therapies compare, I asked several friends who are doctors for their direct input into this chapter. They are Dr. Lee Cowden, M.D. of Dallas, Texas (presently on sabbatical to teach and research); Dr. Dan Clark, M.D. of Orlando, Florida; and Dr. M. Nicholas Martin, M.D., ABFP, of Lancaster, Kentucky.

Although the Food and Drug Administration (FDA) asserts they're trying to protect the interests and well-being of the public, the fact is that they continue to make it difficult and costly to use new, *nontoxic* cancer therapies, while continuing to approve the use of highly potent and toxic chemotherapy drugs.

It remains particularly disturbing that in America right now a fourteen-year-old girl can undergo major surgery for an abortion without her parents' knowledge (much less permission), and yet cancer patients cannot choose alternative cancer therapies that pose less harm to their bodies than many "approved" treatments.

The strict guidelines the FDA has imposed on the research and development of new cancer drugs are so stringent that companies must spend between $150 and $350 million to develop new therapies. Of course, smaller, entrepreneurial drug companies can't even begin to think of those kinds of expenditures, leaving only the drug company giants in the market—the *same* companies that are benefiting from the profits of current therapies.

Brushing aside the rhetoric, one can only conclude that money, and not the well-being of patients, to a greater or lesser degree, dictates what will and won't be available on the market.

Dr. Martin adds the following insight into why scientific studies have been so difficult to come by to validate alternative treatments. "In order to understand why a lot of therapies have not been tried to date is to understand the relationship between the academic centers and the corporate centers. For instance, if you tell a professor you would like to do a certain study, he likely would reply, 'I don't know where I can get the money.' But if you suggest using a drug from a certain corporation (for the study), he knows where he can get the money."

In his book *The Cancer Industry: The Classic Exposé on the Cancer Establishment,* Ralph Moss basically suggests that the pharmaceutical companies have been in collusion with some of the big cancer treatment centers in the country and that they are out to disprove all *effective* natural cancer therapies. Naturally, the big drug companies don't want competition, and the easiest way to undermine any new effective treatments is to get some well-funded medical school to prove the treatments don't work.

If all this sounds farfetched, listen to this. First of all, a finding leading to cancer and to a cause is not the same. What if I told you that both the cause and the theoretical remedy for cancer were discovered back in the 1920s by a German scientist?

CANCER'S THEORETICAL REMEDY
WAS DISCOVERED IN THE 1920S

The German scientist, Oscar Warburg, won *two* Nobel prizes for his work in cell research. His studies of human cells uncovered two common factors in the appearance of cancer. First, according to Dr. Warburg, cancer patients have an imbalance of *ph* in their muscle tissue, meaning there's too much acidity in their systems. With their *ph* out of balance in their bodies over a period of time, Dr. Warburg theorized that those cells become susceptible to transformation into cancer cells. Yet, his findings are not being taught in American medical schools today. Could it be that the priority of the established medical world rests with profits rather than patients?

Dr. Martin is not aware of anyone who has tested the hypothesis that the correcting of *ph* would lead to a cure. Removal of toxins is another story. In most cases, merely changing the environment that is thought to have caused the cancer does not reverse the cancer.

Known causes of the transformation to cancer cells are mostly nutritional. Severe vitamin A deficiencies are brought on by chemicals that deplete vitamin A. Inadequate levels of zinc, B6, folate, and deficiency of vitamin A all depress the genes responsible for controlling cancer. Unless a patient can restore the *ph* balance once again, like dominoes, the cancer is prone to spread and overtake the body.

Next, Dr. Warburg observed that cancer patients also have an unusually high build-up of toxins—literally poisons—within their bodies. The reason for this is a simple genetic fact that people with a certain enzyme convert precancerous chemicals to cancer chemicals and do not have a detoxification enzyme, leading to a buildup of toxins.

He discovered that when the body can no longer fight the pollutants within its own systems, weak cells in the body are prone to being transformed into cancer cells. Since his discovery, medical science has discovered that the toxins work (through enzymes) to deplete nutrition, especially vitamin A.

Just picture how nasty your home would become if the sewer pipes were constantly clogged up. That provides a clue of what may be happening inside your body. When your liver, kidneys, and skin become overwhelmed with toxins in your system, they simply cannot process all their work. When this scene is repeated over a long period of time, the toxins literally pollute your body, setting the stage for a variety of illnesses to creep in.

At one time, the medical world validated and even applauded Dr. Warburg's findings.[1] Yet the majority of doctors graduating from medical schools in America are not taught this approach to cancer treatment.

Understanding Dr. Warburg's findings did not lead to or explain methods of detoxification or the needed replacement of nutrition. By restoring the *ph* balance in the body and helping it to detoxify itself, a person's own body could fight off the aggressive cancer cells . . . and win!

The truth is, *the majority of people* have cancer cells floating throughout their bodies, but because they have healthy immune systems the cells cannot establish a foothold and take over. Cancer cells are able to establish a beachhead when acidic levels within the blood or muscle tissues become too high or when toxins simply build up over a long period of time.

This theory may sound too simplistic to accept, but people should understand that toxins build up because they take them in faster than they can detoxify the chemicals. People who get cancer have enzyme deficiencies or have converting enzymes that subject them to cancer by converting precancerous chemicals to cancer-causing chemicals.

If Doctor Warburg has been correct all along, the obvious question on my mind is, "Why isn't this being taught in American medical schools?" The answer, simply, is money. The pharmaceutical companies in America have a huge vested interest in pushing their drugs, which yield billions of dollars in annual profits.

And what's the connection between the drug companies and medical schools? Again, money is the answer. Guess who provides the majority of funding for research grants in the medical schools across America? That's right, the drug companies. And it's certainly not in their best financial interests to pursue some inexpensive alternative therapy that might work. Such a step would cut too deeply into their profits.

I think the problem boils down to greed: the simple love of money. Paraphrased as the golden rule of cancer therapy research, we could summarize the situation like this: He who has the gold makes the rules.

This is not new information. *Racketeering in Medicine* by J.P. Carter exposes this ingrown scheme.

The result is that medical students are never taught methods of treating cancer, other than the "big three" treatments: chemotherapy, radiation, and surgery. And it is a criminal offense for doctors to engage in medical treatments that lack FDA approval, which is the case for a great many alternative cancer therapy treatments.

Dr. Cowden told me that, as a result, a great many doctors find themselves in quite an ethical bind. Do they, as they promised in their Hippocratic oath, keep the priority of seeking the health and well-being of their patients? Do they take the risk of being jailed here in the United States, or being fined by the FDA, or losing their medical licenses?

Remember, many of these doctors have spent more than a decade in their preparation to practice medicine and many are still tens of thousands—some *hundreds* of thousands—of dollars in debt. Many elect to remain quiet, sticking to what they were taught in medical school, where they learned to dismiss the field of alternative cancer treatments as "quackery."

Dr. Cowden added that most oncologists stick to surgery, chemotherapy, and radiation as the only options available. Some literally don't know any better. Others are motivated by their own financial gain and, frankly, use fear tactics to get their patients to do what they want. "Choose anything other than these three choices, and you'll die," they say. What they don't say is that chemotherapy and radiation can kill just as readily as the actual cancer.

I asked Dr. Dan Clark about the toxicity of chemotherapy and he reflected, "How can you cure cancer with poison? When you read about [the chemotherapy drugs], every one of them causes cancer." He went on to explain that although these powerful drugs do kill cancer cells they also wreak havoc within the body. "They cause a destruction of the intestinal tract lining, cause damage to liver cells, interfere with the endocrine gland function, cause sterility, and weaken the immune response. It's true that chemotherapy will kill tumor cells, but you end up destroying the phase I and II liver enzyme that's responsible for detoxification. So how can that work? It's illogical."

That's exactly what happened to Jackie Kennedy Onassis. She walked into a hospital in New York, and although she had suffered from lymphoma for an extended period of time, she still looked relatively healthy. Three days later she was dead. Lymphoma doesn't take a person out that quickly. What happened? The doctors gave her massive, and what proved to be lethal, doses of chemotherapy. Jackie Onassis died of acute poisoning from chemotherapy.

Let me hasten to add that most physicians who practice alternative therapies also believe there is a place for chemotherapy and/or radiation treatments. This should not be seen as an either/or type of issue. For instance, Dr. Cowden said that if he were an oncologist and had a female patient with a lump in her breast, he likely would perform a lumpectomy and prescribe some limited doses of chemotherapy—combined however, with the active ingredients in the aloe vera plant. He said it has been his observation that this combination only requires one-fifth to one-tenth of the typical chemotherapy dosage—but still yields the same results.

Dr. Clark agreed that, despite its drawbacks, there may be times when limited amounts of chemotherapy may be useful. "There are certain types of tumors that respond beautifully to chemo, but you don't need as much of it. Hodgkin's disease is one: The key is only taking a short regimen, thereby limiting the poison effects. Radiation may be beneficial if small areas are targeted, rather than a larger focus. Antioxidants should be given simultaneously to counter the excessive free radicals produced."

Dr. Clark went on to share the following story. "A number of years ago a physician friend of mine asked for a recommendation to help a friend of his with lung cancer. Subsequent exams revealed a tumor about the size of a grapefruit in his right lung. Although the man was wary of taking chemotherapy, he was open to radiation treatments. When first examined by a radiotherapist, he was told that radiation would only reduce the tumor by a fourth or a third of the size.

"We placed him on an aggressive detoxification program, including phytotheraphy, homeopathics, vitamin C, enzymes, vitamin A, and all the antioxidants," recalled Dr. Clark.

"Over a two-month period, the tumor entirely disappeared. The guy was doing very well. The radiotherapist acknowledged that there was no way the radiation could have made the entire tumor disappear.

"The oncologist talked the man into taking chemotherapy, saying that it would kill any remaining cancer cells left in his body. They did a mega-chemotherapy treatment on him and it killed him. The man died two days after the chemo dose, and his cancer had been eliminated by the radiation and his own immune response. That's so sad."

Dr. Martin concurs that there are occasions when chemotherapy, in spite of its detrimental side effects, can be helpful in treating cancer. "For instance, in the case of breast cancer, if you remove the cancer, there are certain cancers that grow in long lines like threads, and you can't feel them and you can't see them on X ray. Yet, we know that if we give those people chemotherapy, a larger number of them survive than those who don't.

"You've got to remember that there are some other possibilities that we're not putting in that discussion. We're only talking about chemo or no chemo. Other possibilities include boosting the immune system with nutrition. One of the things traditional medicine is not doing is looking at the nutritional status of the patient."

An FDA Raid

As an aside, let me say here that I was taking an alternative therapy available in Tennessee. This therapy consisted of an electromagnetic device invented by an acclaimed physicist, who held patents on several other devices. In the process of verifying his invention, this physicist initially started out to design a better cancer detection device—his theory being that cancer is a cell that has a deficiency of some kind and if that deficiency can be recognized, it can be identified. Therefore, cancer can be discovered before it has colonized or formed tumors.

Without going too much into his theory, it is basically that cancer lives in an acidic environment and cancer has a fundamental deficiency in its molecular structure and lacks one or more electrons that other healthy cells have. Also, the cancer lacks what's called the P-53 gene, which is the gene that programs all cells in the body to die at specific times.

Every cell in the body is programmed to die at a very specific time, so the cells don't continue to multiply out of control. Since cancer cells lack this basic P-53 gene, they will continue to multiply out of control; hence, it's called a malignancy.

The theory behind this machine was very simple. Cancer cells are basically positively charged, but healthy cells in the human body are negatively charged and, therefore, if a living organism— a mouse, rabbit, dog, or human—is exposed to an extremely strong positive electromagnetic field while breathing oxygen, the oxygen will liberate a free electron to the cancer cell. The cancer cell, then, picking up that electron, will give off a slightly higher level of energy, so the diagnostic part of this machine will expose a human to a high positive magnetic field through a ring of fixed electromagnets.

Literally, they were put on a conveyor belt and run through a big coil that put out a very strong positive electromagnetic field, while the patient was breathing oxygen. Then the patient was scanned with a device called an ion detector. The theory was that if the cancer being deficient in one electron had picked up an electron, for a short period of time (up to two hours, according to the inventor), it would put out a stronger electromagnetic field or ionization field than healthy cells would.

Therefore, the cancer in the body could be detected, precisely at what level was not yet determined, but certainly at a level, theoretically, that was much smaller than could be detected by traditional methods, such as MRIs, CAT scans, or bone scans.

Through a whole variety of tests on animals, ranging from mice to guinea pigs, the detection part of the device was tested. The inventor took the use of his device one further step and discovered, somewhat by accident, that by exposing the animals with tumors that had been detected through the strong positive magnetic field, he could expose these animals to a very strong negative magnetic field—in other words a magnetic field in which the polarity had shifted from positive to negative that, in fact, he thought somehow could affect the cancer. He theorized that in the presence of a very strong negative magnetic field the cancer cells might be demolecularized into their basic elements, which are primarily protein.

Again, a variety of experiments were being conducted to verify the theory. He actually designed and built a similar device large enough to accommodate a human being.

The device had been proved harmless to smaller animals. The physicist had used it on himself and it did no apparent damage to him. Understand that the magnetic field that he was using was only a fraction as powerful as that used in an MRI machine, and they're used on tens of thousands of patients on a daily basis, so the physicist felt there was virtually no risk.

Unfortunately, either through ignorance or otherwise, he began accepting terminally ill cancer patients as test subjects before FDA investigative device permits were sought. (He later told me the potential costs were prohibitive.) As word got out, this physicist found himself with cancer patients knocking on his door—many of whom had been given up by the medical system—asking if he could help them. Not having the heart to turn them away, he began to treat patients.

A Christian friend of mine who had been working with this physicist on another project—a machine to process household garbage into usable products—heard about this machine to treat cancer and, to make a long story short, ended up buying the patent rights to the machine to produce and manufacture them. The machine was moved to a small town in Tennessee, where this friend of mine has a manufacturing facility and, again, when the patients found out where the machine was located, they followed it there.

My friend, not having the heart to turn them away either, continued to treat them, at no cost, and had actually hired a full-time nurse at his own expense to operate the machine. The exact efficacy, in other words the effectiveness of the machine, was unknown, since no true clinical testing had been done at this point.

Through the advice of a variety of attorneys and consultants to the FDA and the CDC that I recommended to my friend, they decided to apply for an investigative-device permit from the FDA, even though the theory was, or the thought was, that this machine would not be regulated by the FDA since similar machines were used to treat pain in physical therapy clinics throughout the country. However, in the interest of peace, they decided to file for a permit.

I personally had been treated on this machine several times and, though I didn't have any visible tumors, I did have some indication that the machine was helping me. For example I had a severe back pain for several months, and one of my concerns was that perhaps it was colonized cancer cells—a tumor if you would—that was not yet large enough to detect on traditional scanning devices.

Having been run through the machine the first time as a diagnostic tool, it indicated inflammation in that area. Whether this was actually cancer is unknown because it was an unproven device, being used experimentally, but after several treatments on the machine, the pain in my back disappeared.

I was at this particular facility for about five or six days before I left, planning to come back in about three weeks and be treated again. In the meantime, while I was gone, the Food and Drug Administration, along with state and local authorities, raided the facility where this machine was located, leaving behind them a federal court summons. The charges were operating harmful devices without a permit, extorting money from patients, and using unapproved medical devices for the treatment of cancer.

As of the date of this writing, this case has not come to court, but let me share the bottom-line facts, since I know all the parties involved at this point (at least I know the friend that bought the patent and who was bearing the cost). Number one, he never solicited a single patient. All the patients sought him out and begged him to treat them on the machine. It was explained to them that it was totally experimental. They all signed waivers knowing that it was totally experimental.

It did no harm to anybody as best we can tell. It certainly didn't do harm to me and I used it multiple times. I have a good friend who went through it for more than forty hours with no negative effect and, in fact, he had a melanoma of the lung that now appears to be nothing but scar tissue. In other words, it is at least possible that the active tumor is either in remission or is dead.

The friend who owns the patents and was operating this facility never charged anybody a dime. As a matter of fact, he let them stay in a home that he owned at his expense and even paid, for the first couple of months until he learned better, their long-distance telephone calls amounting to $700 or $800 per month while they called their families.

The device appears to be totally harmless to the human body, and my friend was essentially treating cancer patients who had been given up by traditional medicine and told there was nothing else that could be done for them.

Now, into this picture comes the U.S. government, in the form of the FDA, acting on an anonymous complaint. Without sitting down to talk to the parties involved, the government agency simply rallied the riot troops, raided the facility, confiscated the equipment and all the paperwork, roared off, and filed charges against these people in federal district court in Chattanooga, Tennessee.

Even if the charges come to nothing, and I believe that they will because I know the true facts, thousands of thousands of dollars in legal expenses will have been spent and the patients who were being treated by these machines are no longer being treated. As of this date, four have since died from the cancer or from the previous treatments they had incurred, including chemotherapy, bone-marrow transplants, and radiation.

My question is, isn't this still a free country? And shouldn't consenting adults, who have the ability to choose and are willing to sign waivers, be allowed to choose the therapies they want, provided those therapies can be shown to be no more harmful than the traditional therapies now being used by the medical society and provided they are within the cost-range of the traditional therapies that are being offered?

Bear in mind that I had very good treatment and excellent doctors, and yet it still cost me in the range of $12,000 per day at a traditional medical facility. And, provided that these treatments can show that they would do no additional harm to the body, which is a requirement and a standard actually higher than the standards that are now being used for traditional therapies, shouldn't an American citizen have the right to make that decision for himself or herself?

A 14-year-old girl can walk into an abortion clinic in America, have an abortion that she might die from that day, and it's still legal to give another abortion. And yet, an adult cancer patient does not have the right to choose a therapy that would otherwise be available to him or her outside of this country, and the doctors or the individuals (as in this case, investors) who were willing to put up the money and take all the risks also risk going to jail for several years, have several hundred thousand dollars in fines, and have had their reputations ruined, simply because they were willing to help people with cancer. It doesn't seem very fair to me.

They Did It Again

Let me share with you another story that was told to me by an attorney who is a member of my board of directors. In 1993, a physician in Atlanta, Georgia, a member of the American Medical

Association and a cardiologist from Emory University, invented a machine that he was going to use to treat cancer. In essence, the machine took the blood out of a patient's body; ran it through a recirculation unit; heated the blood to 106 to 108 degrees, which would then kill all the viral infections in the body; recooled the blood and put it back into the body of the patient. He'd used this device on several patients with minor illnesses, with a high degree of success, operating under the experimental device permit from the Food and Drug Administration.

Another friend working at the same university was asked if he thought the device would work on AIDS. As you know, AIDS is a disease of the immune system, caused primarily by a mutant retrovirus and has virtually no cure or even treatment. The doctor replied that he didn't know, but he was willing to experiment.

So a terminally ill AIDS patient was provided to this doctor and went through the same procedure: recycling the blood through an external heating machine, then cooling it back down and putting it into the patient's body. The effect was that the patient showed no HIV indications subsequent to the treatment.

With that success in mind, a second patient was provided, and the same procedure was repeated with the same results. During that procedure, the anesthesiologist who assisted was so impressed by what he saw that he spread the word. He called one of the local newspapers and one of the local television stations in Atlanta and explained what the doctor had done—that it was a revolution in AIDS treatment and a potential cancer treatment as well.

Then, in a few weeks, according to my friend the attorney, this doctor's office was raided by a combination of the FDA and local law enforcement agencies. The machines were confiscated, the property itself and all the records were confiscated, and this doctor's license was suspended. Pressure was brought to bear, to force this doctor to recant any involvement that he'd had with the machine.

According to the attorney, the doctor who invented the machine was pressured to sign a statement that the device was fraudulent and would not work on other patients. The threat behind that was the loss of his medical license for the rest of his life. The physician who had referred the two patients was pressured under the same threat: If he did not sign a document stating that these two patients did not have AIDS but in fact had cat-scratch fever, his medical license would also be denied and he could no longer practice medicine within the United States.

The doctor who invented the machine was fired from his position with the research university on the alleged threat of withdrawal of research funds from the university; and the second doctor was threatened with the loss of his license until he recanted.

I have no personal, firsthand knowledge of these events, but I know my board member very well. He's an honest, ethical man, and he represented the doctor who invented this machine and assures me that the scenario that I just explained to you did, in fact, happen. He agrees that if he hadn't been there, he would not have believed it either. I would not have believed what happened to the people in Tennessee, except, I was a part of it.

These are just two of many horror stories of what has occurred throughout the United States. In my opinion, it's time we put a stop to it and reasserted our rights as American citizens to choose the treatment we want, as long as we're knowledgeable, consenting adults.

The Basic Difference Between
Conventional and Alternative Therapies

Conventional therapies see cancer as an infection within the body. The approach to treatment is to introduce outside elements—chemotherapy, radiation, or surgery—to kill the bad cells. The assumption is that the body does not have the capacity to respond to the challenge within. Although each of these three treatments has a place in the overall plan of treating cancer, each also has costly side effects as previously outlined.

Alternative therapies, however, see cancer as the result of an imbalance within the body's systems. Dr. Warburg's research indicated that the two problem areas were the *ph* imbalance in the body and the inability of the body to rid itself of toxins. By restoring these balances, the body no longer is a good host for cancer cells, and they are naturally eradicated by the body's own defense system. The theory is that *healthy bodies can heal themselves of cancer.*

Dr. Warburg's research of *ph* imbalance and toxic accumulation is now explained with the recent discovery of enzymes that convert nontoxic chemicals to toxins and enzymes that detoxify toxic chemicals that normally break down the nutritional state of the body.

The philosophical differences in these two approaches to cancer treatment lead to misdirected efforts with thousands of patients. First of all, most oncologists plan their treatment for a patient based on how large the tumor is, rather than the actual presence of cancer in the tumor. According to Dr. Cowden, this is a serious mistake, illustrated in the following story he shared with me.

A fifty-three year old woman visited her pulmonary specialist because she was coughing up blood. Her history revealed that she had smoked two packs of cigarettes a day for the past twenty-five or thirty years. The doctor sent her to get a chest X ray, which revealed a golf-ball sized tumor in the upper lobe of her right lung. The tumor was subsequently biopsied and proved to be malignant.

The recommendation of the pulmonary specialist was for the woman to have the tumor removed surgically, followed by a regimen of chemotherapy or radiation, or perhaps both. Because the woman had seen her own mother die a painful death from cancer after these same kinds of treatments, she chose none of the above. Instead, she visited a nutrition counselor in Dallas and asked him, "If you had this condition, what would you do?"

He replied, "I can't tell you what to do, but here's what *I* would do if it were me." And the man made a number of suggestions: stop smoking, change of diet, and take supplemental nutrients.

Two weeks later, the woman's children learned of her condition and began to insist that she have the surgery, a suggestion that she resisted for another two weeks. Finally, after a total of four weeks had passed since initiating nutritional therapy, the woman gave in to the pressure of her children and agreed to the surgery.

When the upper lobe of her right lung was sent to the pathology lab, all the doctors were amazed at what they discovered. After slicing and dicing the tumor from every angle, *not a single live cancer cell could be found.* The natural nutritional therapy helped the woman's body fight off and kill cancer cells and, in some cases, it works very quickly. Obviously each person is different and each case must be assessed individually.

This story illustrates that the size of the tumor does not necessarily reflect the amount of cancer in the body. Oncologists typically use scanning equipment to determine how much more radiation or chemotherapy to give, but what is that based on? *The size of the tumor.* Generally the plan is to continue fighting the tumor with radiation or with massive doses of chemotherapy until the tumor shrinks, dies, or *until the patient cannot accept any additional toxins.*

This simply points out that the size of a tumor cannot be the sole factor in determining how long a regimen of chemotherapy or radiation lasts. Indeed, the cancer cells may already be destroyed, as was the case with this particular woman.

STEPS YOU CAN TAKE

Based on Dr. Warburg's findings, the same steps that will help you prevent cancer will also help you to recover from a malignancy. In other words, if you don't have cancer right now, taking these steps will help you to reduce your risk of cancer in the future. If you already have cancer, these steps will help your body to get back in balance once again.

According to Dr. Cowden, the wide array of cancer treatments, traditional or otherwise, will not help without first restoring a balanced *ph* system in your body.

Healthy Diet

Ninety percent of Americans have too much acidity in their bloodstreams, ranging from mild cases to acute levels. One of the chief causes of this condition comes from eating foods that produce acids: meats, dairy, and grains. Foods that we're allergic to also can trigger a release in our white blood cells that results in high acidity levels in our blood and muscle tissue. But, on the other side, allergy is seldom present without a marked nutritional deficiency.

In contrast, most vegetables and fruits do not result in these high acidity levels in the bloodstream. It is important to eat foods that have a minimal amount of preservatives added and no pesticides, if possible. The no-pesticide approach can be accomplished by doing organic gardening.

The key is to return to a balanced, healthy diet in order for your body's immune system to function at an optimal level. Dr. Clark estimates that as many as 40 percent of cancer patients die as a result of malnutrition.

Good nutrition is not an automatic result of eating a lot of good food. "If I were in my office right now," remarked Dr. Martin, "I could easily pull 200 charts and show you 200 people who have poor nutrition who work every day, look pretty healthy, and their only complaint is fatigue or some other vague complaint. They have depleted energy, they're developing more fungus growth in their mouths (their tongues are turning white more often), and they have multiple toenails with fungus growing on them.

"When these signs occur, any physician who has an elementary understanding of immunity would know something's wrong with the T-cell immunity. The problem is one of two major areas of deficiency: They either suffer from a marked nutritional deficiency or they have reactivated chronic viruses.

"The physician should suggest to the patient that labs be ordered for a nutritional evaluation. The labs I order are CBC, zinc, selenium, liver, vitamin A, beta carotene, B6 folate, and chem-24, including a serum iron. This is not a complete assessment, only a sampling of certain categories of our nutrition."

Exercise

It's likely that you've heard the encouragement to exercise

because it's good for your health, but perhaps you've never understood exactly how good exercise can help your body fight off cancer.

The first thing exercise helps you to do is expand your lungs, thus increasing your oxygen intake. Oxygen selectively kills cancer cells, which are generally anaerobic (oxygen deficient). On the other hand, increased levels of carbon dioxide provide a fertile environment for cancer cells.

With that in mind, picture a person walking briskly for a half an hour each day, compared to a couch potato taking shallow breaths several times a minute. Which person intakes the most antioxidants (cancer fighting agents)? Of course, the person who is exercising. Breathing hard, when incorporated regularly into your lifestyle, helps you to fight cancer.

Dr. Martin says, "Exercise improves your nutrition. If your energy needs are three plates of food a day while being a couch potato and five plates while exercising and each plate has 50 percent nutritionally helpful food, then the exercising has improved your total available nutrition by 77 percent. This does not imply that exercising alone can create the climate for adequate nutrition. People have their own unique needs and their own unique food choices. But for many who choose good food and exercise, this can be adequate for a season of their life."

Exercise also massages your lymph vessels, causing them to constrict and empty their stagnant, toxic materials into the bloodstream, where they can be removed by the kidneys, liver, and skin. Think of those lymph vessels as the little sewer pipes of your body. If they get stopped up or fail to move waste through them, toxic substances build up, stagnate, and ultimately become a receptive host for cancer cells.

Exercise keeps waste moving through those lymph vessels. In addition, we typically perspire when we exercise, allowing impurities to be emitted through the pores of our skin via sweat and oil. Isn't it amazing how God masterfully designed our bodies to cleanse themselves from the inside out?

Reduce Chronic Stress

Everybody encounters stress from time to time in life. There's no way to get around it. However, some people live day in and day out with stress levels at a fever pitch, which can do great damage to your body's immune system. Stress is your body's reaction to a perceived threat of some sort. Some studies suggest that chronic stress can result in a condition in which your body releases hormones that restrict the flow of blood to tissues in the body. Diminished blood flow means less oxygen to your body's tissues and more build-up of carbon dioxide, setting a fertile scene in which cancer cells can prosper.

Spiritual Dimensions of Recovery

Nearly all the doctors I have talked to, who treat the whole person, underscore the spiritual dimensions of both coping and recovering from cancer. There are three dimensions: *keep maintaining hope, have a positive attitude, and seek God's assistance in managing powerful human emotions.*

Maintaining hope is critical, even when a person's future looks very, very bleak. When questioned, oncologists may offer something like, "Ninety percent of the people who have this type of cancer are dead within three months." The patient usually *hears* that, whether the doctor meant that precisely, and he or she will be gone in three months. Outside of all the biochemical factors noted earlier in this chapter, a hopeful attitude is the next most critical predictor of a person's recovery from cancer.

Dr. Cowden also believes that cancer patients need God's help in managing their emotions during a recovery. He told me, "I've never seen a person recover from cancer who had unresolved anger in his or her life, especially if the anger is directed toward God. Nor have I seen people recover from unresolved grief or paralyzing fear. If these emotions are running rampant in patients' lives, they must find a way to get them under control if they expect to get over cancer."

This is precisely where the church can be of so much service to those wrestling with terminal illnesses, since the body of Christ possesses a core faith in God. The Christian faith becomes the foundation from which these powerful human emotions of anger, grief, and fear can be resolved. And the church not only has been given the power of God to minister in this fashion, but we also have the responsibility before God to do so.

Take the emotion of fear, for instance. In the Bible, God repeatedly speaks words of assurance to His people with the words, *"Fear not!"* There's a reason for that. Most of the time, people get caught up in fear because Satan first plants a seed in their minds. Left unchecked, fears begin to mushroom larger and larger, to the point that reality becomes distorted. Underlying many fears is the lie from Satan that God no longer loves us, that He isn't trustworthy, or that something greater than Him can overpower us.

God's word states precisely the opposite: *"Nor any other created thing, shall be able to separate us from the love of God"* (Romans 8:39). So you see how faith becomes the answer to fear. How nice it would be if the battle against these powerful emotions, such as fear, anger, or grief, could be settled, and we'd never again be bothered with them. Instead, we have to walk each day, and even every minute of every day, in faith, trusting God one moment at a time.

For these reasons, when a person discovers that he or she has a terminal illness, I really believe members of the church should meet with that person and pray a hedge of protection over them. As ambassadors from the pit of hell, Satan's demonic hosts are cruel and rejoice in suffering, pain, and terror. Many Christian teachers suggest that an entire demonic realm can be unleashed at the news of cancer.

Dr. Cowden tells a remarkable story of visiting a friend in the hospital who had terminal lymphoma, at least according to his doctors. Dr. Cowden said, "As I entered the room, I felt a distinct presence of death and demonic influences." The man was laying back in the bed, with his head propped up at about a thirty-degree angle. "When I looked into his eyes, there was no life in there; they were empty. His skin was pale blue in color, and his breathing was irregular.

"As a physician, it would have been easy to agree with my friend's doctors, that he would indeed be gone within the next twenty-four hours. But we sat down and prayed over our desperately ill friend and, as we prayed, we asked God to remove the power and the spirit of death from that hospital room. As we prayed, we watched this fellow's face change from lifeless eyes to eyes full of life, and his skin was changed from pale blue to a bright pink. How we praised God for the change!"

Dr. Cowden recommends a book called the *Celebration of Healing* by Emily Gardner-Neil that documents thirty years of her experiences of seeing people having spontaneous healings of their cancer from God. He may choose to do that in your situation or in mine; that is totally God's decision. I trust those answers are caught up in His sovereign wisdom.

There's one thing for sure: To understand the spiritual dimensions of recovery implies taking responsibility for our actions. By that, I mean it's not wise to make poor choices in regard to lifestyle, lack of exercise, and diet, and then expect God to bail us out supernaturally when we become ill.

Open your Bible to Matthew and read about Satan's encounter with Jesus as He stood on the pinnacle of the Temple. The tempter challenged Jesus saying, *"If you are the Son of God, throw Yourself down; for it is written, 'HE WILL GIVE HIS ANGELS CHARGE CONCERNING YOU'; and 'ON their HANDS THEY WILL BEAR YOU UP, LEST YOU STRIKE YOUR FOOT AGAINST A STONE'"* (Matthew 4:6).

Jesus knew better. He recognized the deception of Satan's enticement and responded with this truth, *"On the other hand, it is written, 'YOU SHALL NOT PUT THE LORD YOUR GOD TO THE TEST'"* (Matthew 4:7).

Live your life responsibly. Don't live a lifestyle that's conducive to causing cancer or some other terminal illness and then get angry with God if He doesn't bail you out. Although Dr. Cowden and others have seen spontaneous healings by the power of God, they wouldn't recommend that you live irresponsibly in the hopes that God will provide that for you at the last minute.

Note to the reader: This chapter is composed of material either written or dictated by the doctors mentioned within the chapter.

1. Anne E. Frahm with David J. Frahm, *A Cancer Battle Plan* (Piñon Press: Colorado Springs CO) p 31.

CHAPTER ELEVEN

What To Do When Your Money Runs Out

*F*ighting for physical well-being is only one-half the battle against cancer. Paying for medical treatment is a completely different struggle. And quite frankly, skyrocketing hospital and doctor bills can wedge family members into a crushing bind. On the one hand, who doesn't want their loved ones to have the best medical treatment money can buy? On the other, nearly every family has at least one person who is money-wise and feels the burden of mounting debts for medical care. These factors, which some families find difficult to discuss openly, may trigger tensions, arguments, and bitterness precisely at a time when the family unit needs to pull together.

As I have often said, how people manage their money is an outward reflection of their spiritual condition and, for that reason, mounting medical bills can unleash a wide range of emotions. Keep in mind that the emotional atmosphere surrounding cancer itself is often highly charged and volatile already. Nerves often are frayed as daily routines are scrapped, sleep is often hard to come by, meals are skipped, and tensions mount. Mushrooming debt just compounds the mental pressure.

It's not hard to understand why families feel overwhelmed and panicky when it comes to medical care and finances. Can you think of another business that has an entrée into your wallet to the tune of tens of thousands of dollars, and there's not much you can do about it? I mean, if you take your car into the shop for repair, you get an estimate up front. If you need repair work done on your home, you get an estimate and then decide if you can afford to proceed. Even if you're paying for your child's college education, you still have a pretty firm idea in advance of how much you'll be paying.

Medical care is different. Once you sign in at the hospital, it's like signing a blank check. You don't know with any degree of certainty what you'll eventually get into. The unexpected always seems to happen. One test can trigger an entirely different line of treatment than originally proposed. A simple operation, followed by complications, can lead to days in ICU. And a family's financial future can literally hinge on the outcome of a test or operation. Insurance is fine, but most of it only pays a portion of the total bills.

All of this is to say that the financial aspects of medical care are critically important aspects that must be addressed forthrightly by your family. It's not an issue that can be ignored. Someone, somewhere along the line, will have to deal with it. This chapter is committed to helping you to respond to that challenge. The following principles offer a first step toward maintaining your financial sanity—and integrity—when facing catastrophic medical bills.

THE ENORMOUS COSTS OF CANCER TREATMENT

When you check into a hospital, assume you will pay an average of $4,000 to $6,000 per day, and that doesn't include the treatment. If you require specialized treatment, such as surgery, your bill may well average $10,000 to $12,000 per day over a seven-day period. Suppose you have cancer of the bladder, resulting in a five-day stay in the hospital. With all associated expenses added in, you're going to spend $50,000 to $60,000 before you leave. Some people take thirty years to pay off a home mortgage of that amount. Like it or not, that's where medical care in America is right now.

Although a good health insurance policy will pay the largest portion of the bill, it is virtually guaranteed that you will be left with some outstanding debt. I've seen families exhaust a million dollar limit on their insurance policy—particularly when cancer is involved. That can happen easily, for instance, if a child has leukemia and requires chemotherapy for extended periods of time. At that point you have to decide what your obligation is. It is unconscionable that families are plunged into financial ruin by circumstances totally beyond their control—even with insurance coverage.

A growing number of people have no health insurance at all. If your first thoughts turn to the extremely poor and indigent, think again. In our society those living below the poverty level are cared for very well by government programs. Medicaid often will pay 100 percent to the best hospitals, 100 percent to the doctor, and 100 percent of the pharmacy bill.

Those who are presently experiencing the devastating blows of unpaid medical bills are middle-class Americans who make too much to qualify for government assistance but not enough to tackle the enormous debts.

Unfortunately, the hospital bill is only one part of the financial equation. On top of that, doctor bills and the cost of prescription medicines are added, both of which can cause the debt to soar. When our son Dan was in the hospital, at one time he had over thirty doctors caring for him. Can you imagine what it was like to simply keep all of those bills organized, much less think about paying them?

Lost wages during an extended recuperation also can add stress to the family, particularly if the patient is self-employed. Suppose you are self-employed as a carpenter or as a business consultant. If you're not working, your business income evaporates, and your family either has to dip into savings or seek support from outsiders. Most churches will help initially with food, child care, and perhaps even a house payment or car payment for a while.

But all too often those resources tend to dry up long before the needs do. It is important to let your needs be known, however, so others can respond. And if your church can't help, circulate news of your needs among your friends. You may be surprised at how God can provide through what might seem to be the least likely sources.

There's no secret to this whatsoever. It just takes commitment on the part of God's people to someone else's needs being every bit as important as our own needs and having a willingness to do unto others as we would want them to do unto us.

The possibility of being partially or totally disabled must be considered as a long-term side effect of cancer treatment. If you're unable to return to your livelihood as a result of surgery or subsequent treatments, you need to promptly apply for Social Security disability. If you don't have a personal disability policy, start the paperwork for Social Security benefits immediately. The longer you wait, the longer it will take for them to process your claim.

Normally Social Security disability benefits won't begin paying until you have been disabled for at least a year. Even most personal disability policies have a waiting period of two weeks to three months before they will pay. *For this reason, I strongly encourage all families to build up an emergency fund of at least three to six months of salary.*

If it appears that you're going to permanently be disabled and no other resources are available, then you also will need to apply for whatever financial aid may be offered by state agencies. I don't like welfare, but one legitimate use is for when a debilitating illness is involved.

Generally speaking, if you have insurance you're going to be treated with great consideration by the doctors and the hospital, simply because they know they're going to get their money. They may not get everything they bill for, but at least they'll get a sizeable portion of it. If you don't have insurance, you'll likely encounter some resistance to obtaining all the medical treatment you may want. After all, the medical professionals may well try to minimize their losses if they know you are going to have trouble paying their bills.

For that reason, it's important to know what your patient rights are. For instance, any nonprofit hospital or hospital that receives federal funding is *required to treat you.* They cannot refuse treatment because you can't pay for their services. That's not necessarily true of a doctor unless he or she works for the hospital. Most doctors' offices are private enterprises and, as such, the doctors are not required to treat you. Most honorable practitioners will provide their services.

For every doctor who refuses treatment to indigent patients there are a hundred who will because they are so faithfully committed to their oaths. There are thousands of excellent doctors in America who have deep, godly motivations for their work. You just have to let your needs be known. Somewhere within your circle of contacts God has a physician who understands your particular illness and who will do whatever you need to have done without regard for money. Those who won't, in my opinion, should be in another profession.

TWO ATTITUDES TO KEEP
WHEN THE BILLS MOUNT UP

Be Honest with Your Doctors, Hospitals, and Church Family

Lay out your situation up front, even before your surgery or treatment, especially if you don't have insurance. Don't be bashful; just be honest and tell those who will do the work that you don't have the money to pay for all the costs.

As I said earlier, public hospitals that receive government funds are required by law to treat you, so they can't turn you away. But being honest will enhance your integrity, even if you don't have the means to pay your bill. And who knows? There may be a Christian doctor who says, "Hey, I'm willing to do it, and I won't charge you anything." You'll never know unless you're honest about your needs.

Following my son's automobile accident we were facing a $250,000 hospital bill. He had no insurance, and there was no way I could pay it. Even though the situation seemed hopelessly out of control, God knew what was going on, and He had a plan to meet the need.

We began taking responsibility by requesting an itemized bill. Much to our surprise, after reviewing the bill line by line, the real total dropped from $250,000 to closer to $170,000. When I had paid all that I could, which amounted to a drop in the bucket, God began moving in ways that I could not have anticipated.

One of my close friends from Atlanta, Terry Parker, an attorney, set up a trust fund on his own and then began calling people on our behalf and saying, "You know, the Burketts just can't pay this huge bill. They could just walk away from it, since Dan is twenty-one, but Larry's determined to pay it all off as a testimony to God's faithfulness."

Well, God is faithful. Through Terry's effort, we saw about $100,000 raised toward the balance on the hospital bill. But that wasn't all. In a subsequent interview on Dr. Dobson's radio program, "Focus on the Family," out of the clear blue sky, Dr. Dobson mentioned our need and the rest of the money came in. I know it's very unlikely that God will answer your particular need in the same way He answered mine, but *He is faithful,* nonetheless.

He may even have a more exciting plan for you, partly because His first choice is to work through His own people—the church.

God Is in Control Even When You Are Not

God, our Father, is completely sovereign. That means He ultimately rules whether or not we choose to let Him; He doesn't need our permission. Nothing catches Him by surprise.

He never makes a mistake. He never harbors ill will toward those He loves. He is always faithful to His own and, above all, He will never abandon us (see Romans 8:31–39).

Mushrooming medical bills, coupled with health uncertainties of the future, may leave you in a tailspin, wondering if things will ever settle down to normal again. But no matter how out of control things seem for you, remember that God has not forgotten you. *His grace at work in you is not a function of your performance.* You can't earn His good favor. He loves you and is committed to you already.

One of my favorite Bible passages comes from Mark 4:35–41. The disciples and Jesus were out in a boat on the Sea of Galilee one night. While Jesus slept, a fierce wind arose and the disciples were fearful that they would lose their lives. They felt quite out of control—no question about that. But even then, Jesus had things in complete control, so much so that He continued to sleep.

When the disciples awakened Him, He rebuked the wind and said to the sea, *"Hush, be still."* And here's the best part. *"And the wind died down and it became perfectly calm"* (Mark 4:39).

Let Jesus do the same for you when the emotional and financial tidal waves threaten your peace of mind. In Matthew 28, Jesus declared that *all* authority in heaven and on earth belonged to Him. In faith, let Him exercise His power in your life when things seem so out of control.

WHERE TO FIND HELP

Remembering that God is in control can help you maintain your peace and composure when the medical bills begin to surpass what you are able to pay. God's plan all along may very well be for your needs to be met through the financial surplus that others have built up, as a witness of love to an unbelieving world.

I think that's precisely why the apostle Paul wrote to the Corinthian Christians: *"At this present time your abundance being a supply for their want, that their abundance also may become a supply for your want, that there may be equality; as it is written, 'HE WHO GATHERED MUCH DID NOT HAVE TOO MUCH, AND HE WHO GATHERED LITTLE HAD NO LACK'"* (2 Corinthians 8:14–15).

It's a normal part of God's plan for believers to have their needs met through the surplus of other Christians. To prevent chaos from occurring, God's Word clearly reveals some guidelines to govern when we should appeal to others for help in meeting daily needs. Without these guidelines, a spirit of love and generosity in the church family could quickly be taken advantage of and abused.

These principles suggest that there is a priority of responsibility for having your needs met. When followed, they ensure a sense of balance in the church when it comes to responding to practical needs in love.

You Are Responsible To Do What You Can

Two verses of Scripture are worthy of careful inspection at this point. *"Bear one another's burdens, and thus fulfill the law of Christ"* (Galatians 6:2). Yet, verse 5 of that same chapter says, *"For each one shall bear his own load."* Which is it? Are we to look to our brothers and sisters in Christ to help carry our financial burdens, or are we to stand on our own two feet? Where do you draw the line as to what you're personally responsible for?

The word that is translated as *load* in verse 5 comes from a Greek word used to describe the cargo on a ship. Related words mean something carried, to bear something, or a task to be done. A good illustration would be the knapsack a hiker takes on a trail. On such a trip, every hiker has his or her own knapsack, and it would be unreasonable to ask someone else to carry what is rightfully his or hers to bear.

That's what Paul is saying in this verse. Take care of your own commitments and responsibilities. If you have medical bills, it's your responsibility to pay them if you have the resources.

The word *burdens* in verse 2 translates from a completely differ-ent Greek word, however. The gist of that word suggests going down under an abundant load, or a crushing blow. Related words translate as serious or savage. To use the hiking illustration again, this Greek word implies trying to walk under the weight of a crushing boulder, not a knapsack. Hence the contrast in mean-ings between the two verses.

Paul says you're to mind your own business and take care of your own needs to the extent that God supplies the resources. However, circumstances may develop that are nothing less than a crushing blow: medical bills piling up to the tune of tens of thou-sands of dollars.

That's not uncommon following a stay in the hospital. As I mentioned earlier, it is estimated that an average trip to the hospi-tal will cost between $4,000 and $6,000 *a day* in the United States. Specialized care, such as a coronary care unit or intensive care unit, may run between $10,000 and $12,000 a day.

People can spend more money in two weeks than they can save in a decade. As you might guess, carrying some type of health insurance is the most certain defense against this type of financial assault. If you qualify for medical insurance, you have a responsi-bility to both your family and your church to obtain it and main-tain the policy. Since your responsibility or lack thereof at this point can have major implications for others, your actions are a matter of stewardship. Of course, if you cannot find an insurer who will cover you, there's not much you can do. But that's all God expects of us: to do what we can responsibly do.

However, even if you've done all you can do to protect yourself against catastrophic medical indebtedness, you may still be look-ing at staggering, six-digit medical invoices. In this situation, God still looks for you to "carry your knapsack." Do what you can do, even if that is paying $10 dollars a month toward the bill. All too often in a situation like this Christians pay nothing because they can't pay it all. Pay what you can and then turn to others for help. That leads to the next level of responsibility.

Approach Your Extended Family

Many who are overwhelmed with medical bills and simply don't have the resources turn immediately to the church for help. The Scripture, however, says you should turn *first* to your extended family. A key insight along these lines stems from the apostle Paul's counsel to Timothy regarding the ongoing care for widows in the church.

"Honor widows who are widows indeed; but if any widow has children or grandchildren, let them first learn to practice piety in regard to their own family, and to make some return to their parents; for this is acceptable in the sight of God" (1 Timothy 5:3–4).

The word that translates as *return* suggests respect or support of a tangible nature. This same idea is repeated in the same chapter of 1 Timothy. *"If any woman who is a believer has dependent widows, let her assist them, and let not the church be burdened, so that it may assist those who are widows indeed"* (1 Timothy 5:16).

The word translated as *burdened* in that verse comes from the same root word that is used in Galatians 6:2, where Paul spoke of the *crushing load.* In other words, if you can take care of needs within your family, do that, so the church will not come under a crushing load.

Following the precedent of approaching extended family for help with oppressive medical bills may be awkard or even downright difficult. But God also may use the occasion to convict family members of unrepentant pride, lack of forgiveness, and bitterness, ultimately leading to a healing within fragmented family generations. In God's total plan, the person with the cancer or terminal illness may not be the only person in need of healing.

Nonetheless, there inevitably will be times when the combined resources of both you, your insurance benefits, and your extended family can only scratch the surface on what you owe. When that happens, it is biblical to turn to your church family.

Seek Assistance from Your Church Family

There will be times when Christians in need should approach

their church families for financial assistance. That's totally biblical, and the precedent is seen clearly in Scripture. Impractical? Your first thoughts may be that of standing outside the pastor's office with stacks of medical bills in hand, feeling like a beggar. All too often that's our pride showing through. Just because some abuse the generosity of others does not make sharing a need with your church wrong.

Although most churches can help a family in need with daily living expenses, few are prepared to help with major, catastrophic medical bills. They just don't have the resources. But we would have many more financial resources available if the church would obey God's command of bringing the tithe, the first 10 percent of our income, into the storehouse.

Consider that *the average American church member only gives about 2 percent of his or her income to the church.* If people would give 10 percent of their first fruits to the Lord's work, there would be plenty of money available to help families in need. Just pick up a copy of your church's annual budget, multiply it by five, and discover the resources available for meeting needs, if God's people were simply obedient to tithing.

The truth is, God has already supplied the funds to His church for needs like this. And not just medical bills, but the needs of single parents and paying off building debts as well. It's all there. The reason the needs go unmet is because we, God's people, are mismanaging what God has provided, spending it on our own desires.

The Jews brought nearly *one-fourth* of their incomes to God's storehouse, not just 10 percent. So, again, take your annual church budget and multiply the average church member's gift of 2 percent by about 12.5, and see if you think that amount of money would be sufficient. What a witness that would be to our selfish, materialistic culture. The money is there to meet all the real needs. We just have to shake it loose. Perhaps historians would then remark about our generation, "Behold, how those Christians love one another!"

No, God has no shortage of funds in His economy. Rather, there is a shortage of vision among His people today, and nowhere is that more evident than in our lack of zeal for meeting physical needs within the body of Christ.

The prophet Haggai had stern words for the people of Judah because they put their own selfish needs ahead of the work within God's house: *"Is it time for you yourselves to dwell in your paneled houses while this house lies desolate?" Now therefore, thus says the Lord of hosts, "Consider your ways! You have sown much, but harvest little; you eat, but there is not enough to be satisfied; you drink, but there is not enough to become drunk; you put on clothing, but no one is warm enough; and he who earns, earns wages to put into a purse with holes"* (Haggai 1:4–6).

Haggai's words serve as quite a challenge to the American church today. Ironically, by putting our own priorities first, we never have enough. Our appetites are insatiable. Like the fallen culture around us, if our people fail to provide the necessary resources for new building projects, we borrow it. Who knows how many millions of dollars of God's money is wasted on interest charges to the local banks!

Conversely, when we sacrificially obey God's commands, He will supernaturally multiply our resources, providing nothing less than an abundance. It is the story of the five loaves and two fishes all over again. That should not take us by surprise, since God has already told us that He would respond to our faith and obedience in this manner. (See Malachi 3:10 and Luke 6:38.)

Just as there are immutable physical laws, such as gravity, God has established key economic laws that He blesses, one of which is the law of giving generously. Again, let me state that there is no shortage of funds for God's church to do the things He has called us to. The only shortages we have can be found in faith, vision, and obedience.

This is no little issue for the church of today. We're teetering on the brink of major cutbacks in government social services, which will trigger withdrawal symptoms in our culture, much like an alcohol or cocaine addict's trauma. People on the fringes of society, such as unwanted babies and the elderly, will need care that the government no longer will be able to provide. Churches that have a vision for generous sharing will be raised up by God like a *"city set on a hill [that] cannot be hidden."*

Let me point out another way the church can be of assistance to those in need. Hurting families probably will need someone with the gift of helps to step in and provide some organization to the family's money management: basic things like balancing the checkbook and being sure the bills are paid on time.

I realize those are personal matters, and most people would be reluctant to ask if those needs are being met. But the need is there. Perhaps the pastor or a church leader who is close to the family can tactfully inquire if help is needed in these very practical areas.

Along these lines, I am pleased to say that the CFC ministry has trained more than 15,000 people across the United States to provide practical help like this, and we have more than 1,000 referral counselors in churches right now. If your church doesn't have a trained financial consultant, we'd be happy to train someone who can serve in this capacity. To obtain more information, just call our seminar department at (770) 534-1000 and inquire about our Teacher-Counselor Training program.

Besides financial assistance, the church family can help a victim of cancer or another terminal illness with another adjustment: *vocational rehabilitation.* The fact is, many people can no longer return to their career because of limitations following surgery. In my case, I have limited use of my left arm as a result of my left shoulder blade being removed. Had I been a brick mason or carpenter by trade, I would have had to totally change my means of making a living.

There are two ways the church family can help someone making a career change. First, that person needs some type of career assessment that will highlight his or her potential in new career fields. Career Pathways, a division of Christian Financial Concepts, provides a comprehensive assessment covering personality, skills, vocational interests, and values. Funneling people toward this type of service is a step in the right direction. For more information on Career Pathways, call (770) 534-1000.

Next, the local church can assist someone in a career transition through the services of a career support group. With thousands laid off through the corporate downsizing of the 1990s, many churches have had the heart and vision to assist their members and communities with this type of ministry. You can obtain more information about opening a career support group in your church by contacting the Christian Employment Network in Bellevue, Washington at (425) 455-2512.

HOW TO MINIMIZE YOUR MEDICAL BILLS

It goes without saying that, as a good steward, you should do everything you can to minimize your medical bills, whether you have insurance coverage or not. That doesn't mean you need to bypass needed medical treatments or to get something for nothing. It does mean that you do your best to pay only what you owe, rather than "looking the other way" if your bill is padded with inaccurate charges. Ultimately, someone has to pay: either you, your family, your church family, or the insurance company, which in turn collects higher premiums from policyholders. Review all bills carefully!

Request a Meeting with the Hospital Administrator

Advise him or her of your exact predicament, along with your desire to pay your bills. Insist on meeting with the decision makers, since support staff are apt to say no to your every suggestion.

Don't be afraid to negotiate the bill. Depending on the hospital, as many as one-fourth of the patients may be in default with their bills. Keeping in mind that the hospital is a business, how can they sustain losses of these gigantic proportions? Like anyone else, the losses are passed on to the paying customers. So your total hospital bill is inflated to help cover the losses from other patients. That's why you may be charged $4 for each tongue depressor, $20 for a Tylenol, or some such aberration.

That being the case, don't be afraid to ask the administrator's cooperation in peeling your bill back to the actual costs of your medical care and stay in their facility. After all, you're someone who is committed to paying off your debt rather than avoiding it, and you'll be respected for that.

Request That Collection Agencies Not Be Employed To Collect Your Account

I talked to a cancer patient at a doctor's office not long ago. Like me, he'd been through surgery, but that was followed by a regimen of chemotherapy. Since he didn't have insurance, he owed well over $100,000 when I met him. He and his wife paid what they could, several thousand dollars or so, but not enough to make a real dent on the total debt.

Unfortunately he was being harassed by a collection agency. Typically when a patient can't pay, the account goes into default and from there it is turned over to a collection agency. Frankly many of these groups have developed an attitude that is harsh and insulting. In the first place, the agents assume everyone can pay but simply are unwilling and that a *Rambo*-type approach will help to change people's minds. So they basically start with threatening letters, followed by threats of court action. In fact, they may actually take a debtor to court.

The trick is to preempt this group by leveling with your doctors and with the hospital. Simply ask them not to send your account to collections since it's not going to do any good. After all, you can't squeeze blood out of a turnip. They may do it anyway, if that's the standard policy they follow, but it never hurts to ask.

Once your account has gone to collection, if you live in a state where they have a garnishment law, they can legally attach your wages. That means a negotiated portion of your paycheck is skimmed off the top—much like your federal and state income taxes and Social Security are withheld.

If this happens and the amount awarded is so excessive that it deprives your family of basic necessities and robs all other creditors to the exclusive benefit of just the one, you may have to file for legal bankruptcy protection. Let me hasten to emphasize that what I am advocating is a Chapter 13 reorganization, in which all creditors will be paid, but under court supervision, in which case one creditor cannot wreck your finances. All too often collection companies force creditors into situations that could otherwise be avoided with a little compassion and common sense.

Request an Itemized Bill from Your Doctors and Hospital

Alert them up front that you will need their cooperation in this matter. Administrators usually will be open to working with you on this, since it's in their best interests to minimize potential losses.

As I mentioned before, when we reviewed my son's hospital bill, we dropped the amount due from $250,000 to about $170,000 —*a difference of $80,000!* They charged us, for instance, many times over for the same piece of medical equipment. To keep the swelling down, they had a special "cold" machine to cool Dan down. Often they would bring in one and it wouldn't work, so they would bring in another one. The problem was, the original, broken machine stayed on the bill.

When I looked at the bill, there were sometimes seven or eight machines charged *per day,* and we were there for nearly eighty days. Once a machine was entered on the bill, it never came off. I knew Dan didn't need seven or eight cooling machines per day. Check your bill carefully. Ask questions. Computers make mistakes sometimes.

We negotiated a lot of things with the hospital. We were charged $17 a foot for some plastic tubing. You and I both know plastic tubing, even for a hospital, doesn't cost $17 a foot. When we brought this to the attention of the business office, they graciously agreed to only charge us their actual cost: $.40 a foot.

Have Your Family Keep a Log of Services Rendered

This is a natural follow-up for the point above. Write down what tests and services are rendered daily. Keep a daily log of tests that are run and special treatments to compare with your hospital bills. If you don't, your memory will invariably become foggy and distorted with the passing of time. And in spite of their best efforts, hospitals may bill patients for services never rendered.

WHAT TO DO WHEN THE MONEY RUNS OUT

Don't Worry

What happens if no one helps? What if you make your needs known, but no one says, "Sure, I'll keep your kids," or "I'd be happy to fix supper every Tuesday night," or "Can we help you with your car or house payment?"

The fundamental principle to keep in mind is, don't worry. *Worry is taking on a responsibility that belongs to God.* Just tell the Lord the truth about your circumstance, do the best you can, and trust Him for the outcome. Worry does not add one asset toward solving the problems you face, and it can add many liabilities.

Jesus said, *"Do not be anxious then, saying, 'What shall we eat?' or 'What shall we drink?' or 'With what shall we clothe ourselves?' For all these things the Gentiles eagerly seek; for your heavenly Father knows that you need all these things. But seek first His kingdom and His righteousness; and all these things shall be added to you. Therefore do not be anxious for tomorrow; for tomorrow will care for itself. Each day has enough trouble of its own"* (Matthew 6:31–34).

Don't sacrifice your peace of mind because of worry. God's desire is for you to do what's within your ability to do and then be at peace.

Liquidate Your Assets

If you've stuck money back for an emergency fund, your current situation may very well be just such an emergency. You will compromise your credibility if you ask others to help before you do what you can on your own. You may have to reach into your retirement savings to pay on the debt.

I've been asked about whether people should go as far as selling their home. That's a tough question. I think that's an individual decision on the part of the Christian. You might gain insight from this proverb. *"Do not withhold good from those to whom it is due, when it is in your power to do it. Do not say to your neighbor, 'Go, and come back, and tomorrow I will give it,' when you have it with you"* (Proverbs 3:27–28).

If you took the treatment and they knew in advance that you weren't going to be able to pay, virtually no doctor or hospital is going to ask you to sell your home (assuming it is a reasonably priced home) to pay the bills.

If a person in that situation came to me for counsel, I would encourage him or her not to sell the home just to pay medical bills. Often the situation is taxing enough on finances; being homeless may be too much.

The one thing I would say is, don't jump into bankruptcy as a quick way out. Can you really trust God for the outcome of such a decision that runs so contrary to the norm in our culture?

If You Have To Consider Bankruptcy

Bankruptcy is not the cure-all that many people hope it will be. Even though the legal system formally absolves people in bankruptcy from all their debts, I believe God still says that we are to pay what we owe. In fact, that's exactly what we're told in God's Word. *"When you make a vow to God, do not be late in paying it, for He takes no delight in fools. Pay what you vow! It is better that you should not vow than that you should vow and not pay"* (Ecclesiastes 5:4–5).

Bankruptcy should be considered a last resort, not the first option to be exercised. There are certain circumstances, however, when I believe a Christian should consider filing for bankruptcy protection.

- If you are concerned about the mental health of you or your spouse—by that, I mean a genuine concern of a threat of suicide—bankruptcy may relieve the immediate pressure from creditors. Taking this step may provide you more time to reestablish the equilibrium of your family's cash flow, seek professional counseling, and recuperate from the treatments you've had.

- If it appears that one of your creditors is attempting to lay claim to all of your assets to the exclusion of all others, bankruptcy may ensure an equitable distribution of your remaining assets.

- You may not have a choice. Three or more of your creditors can put you into bankruptcy whether you want to or not.

- If your creditors place pressure on you to break laws or engage in illegal or immoral behavior, bankruptcy may indeed be a step toward preserving your integrity and Christian witness.

For a Christian, bankruptcy is an option only for the purpose of reorganizing a way to repay your creditors. *"The wicked borrows and does not pay back, but the righteous is gracious and gives"* (Psalm 37:21).

When it comes down to it, if you don't have good health insurance, you're going to be obligated for thousands of dollars of expenses. The bottom line is, do the best you can do, as unto the Lord, and trust God. Walk in peace. God doesn't expect you to do things you cannot do, only the things that are within the realm of possibility as you trust Him.

Pay as much as you can, and let your needs be known to those around you, especially within the church. If, in fact, you're attending a church family that is really functioning the way they should, they will step up and help you. If they don't, my suggestion would be to go and find a church family that is responsive.

IF YOU HAVE A SICK FRIEND
If you know someone who is ill, let me encourage you to get

involved on behalf of his or her care. Even if you are told they don't need anything, don't take that as an answer. One of the things that ministered to Judy and to me the most was the care and concern of our friends. I sincerely appreciated those who asked, "Is there anything we can do?" Even though we usually said no, I especially appreciated those who didn't take no for an answer.

For instance, the food our staff delivered each day after I returned home from the hospital was a real godsend. I also appreciated those who came a few weeks later when the mental fatigue factor hit Judy and Kim. Really good friends usually come back long after the crowds leave—and they are *special*.

Most people, just like we did, will decline your offer for help, probably to see if you're serious or just being polite. Our friends just kept coming back, time and time again, not only offering to help but actually finding things to do.

If you stick around your friends, you'll find something that needs to be done, no matter what they say. *"A friend loves at all times"* (Proverbs 17:17). A good friend will push a little bit further when his or her offer to help is declined. You don't want to be obnoxious, but you don't want to be a pushover, either. Get involved. Most people won't produce a list of things they need help with on the first inquiry, but if you gently press a little, there's likely a way you can help. Don't give up!

CHAPTER TWELVE

Time Out!

W hen playing the game of "tag" as a child, I can remember how exhausted and winded we would become after chasing one another. So we invented a rule that when we became too tired to run anymore, we could always call "Time out!" after which we were off limits. No more chasing, no more running, and we couldn't be tagged "it" anymore. The person who claimed "Time out!" could stand on the sideline watching as the others continued chasing and playing until he or she recovered.

At the time, the need for rest and recuperation became very important, and since everyone did it every once in a while there was no stigma. I remember something else about time outs: I could see the whole game better and see who was the fastest runner. So, the time-out person could have a better perspective of the whole game of tag, rather than just a fleeting glimpse while hiding.

When people find themselves in a medical crisis, such as the discovery of cancer, a game of emotional "tag" usually follows. There are people to call, doctors to see, and decisions to be made, usually under stress and in a short period of time. Add to that the clouds of emotion and shock, which typically accompany bad medical news, and the result is confusion—or what I call "systems' overload." That's how I felt, and I needed to take a "time-out" occasionally, just to get away by myself, in an attempt to regain my equilibrium and sort out the impact of what I was facing. I felt like my mind was on overload because it was.

FEELING OVERWHELMED

I *felt* overwhelmed at first because I was. I had to make some major decisions in a very short period of time, based on a limited amount of information. I knew very little about cancer. Yet, before me stood two highly trained doctors, suggesting that I have my kidney and my shoulder blade removed.

What was I supposed to say? I had a twenty-minute appointment with a surgeon who had been looking at my X rays for perhaps ten minutes when he asked me to make a critical, life-changing decision. As for me, I was still reeling at the news that I even had cancer. No wonder I felt overwhelmed; the circumstances *were* overwhelming.

If I had all to do over again, I think I would diffuse these feelings by allowing some time to pass before I made any major decisions. I would stand back and say, "Okay, I've had this cancer for a while . . . maybe up to three years or more. What difference would it make if I waited another month?" Well, now I know it probably wouldn't have made any difference.

Understandably, doctors are very reluctant to speculate on possibilities like that. About the best they can say is, "Well, you might be okay. Then again, you might not be." In my case, the decisions were complicated by the fact that I knew both doctors had worked me into very busy schedules. Once I got out of their schedules I might have a difficult time getting back in.

In retrospect, the wisest thing I could have done after hearing all the options would have been to take a step back, get a grip on the situation, and begin to investigate some alternatives. I needed to get some firsthand knowledge, talk to people who had renal cell carcinoma, and learn more about the surgery and the effects people typically experienced as a result.

What, if any, alternative treatments were available for this? Cancer was a real unknown to me, and many of my anxieties could have been laid to rest with knowledge of the disease. But it was hard to understand what the doctors were telling me because, in large part, they used terms I wasn't familiar with. And knowing that they were busy and had another twenty-five patients lined up in the waiting room only added to the pressure.

I wanted to say, "I don't really understand what you're talking about. What is adenocarcinoma? And what is the exact difference between an adenocarcinoma, melanoma, myeloma, and a lymphoma?" It all sounded very confusing, and I could have used a guide to cancer terminology.

One of the best things any cancer patient could do is to take a time-out, get a medical reference book (like one of those listed in the Appendix), and read it. At least that would have helped me understand the right questions to ask. It probably would be one of the cheapest investments I ever made, especially in light of the ensuing medical bills. But, like I said, I felt the pressure to decide—right then.

I didn't know enough to ask the right kind of questions, and that alone should have triggered an automatic response. As Psalm 37:7 says, *"Rest in the Lord and wait patiently for Him."* But when you're in mental or emotional overload, it's hard to think straight and see clearly. For that reason, I encourage anyone to take the time to thoroughly analyze his or her situation.

You wouldn't buy an automobile the first time you saw it, so don't buy an operation the first time you hear of it. Take time to pray about it. Most doctors are willing to work around your schedule; mine certainly were. Just be sure you understand whether or not there are latent dangers if you wait for another month or so before you proceed.

THE RUSH OF ANXIETY

If feeling overwhelmed is one common feeling, so is experiencing anxiety. By that I mean the way news of a serious illness can throw people into a frantic pace to do things. Emotions become exaggerated. Everything becomes urgent and must be settled immediately. For instance, most oncologists will tell you that many patients literally demand the earliest surgery date possible. News of a terminal illness often can trigger a flurry of activities that tend to minimize, deny, or fix the situation. Unfortunately, usually none of our solutions can remedy or change the truth of what we're really facing.

To illustrate what I mean, I've observed how "religious" people act, following the news of a life-threatening illness. There's a sudden new zeal to get back in the Bible and do all the studying they should have been doing for the past ten years. All the praying they meant to do instantly becomes a priority, and well it should, but you can't make up for lost time. Just realistically start where you are.

Although I've always tried to make Bible study and prayer a regular part of my daily life, I found myself preoccupied totally with "religious" matters. I even caught myself feeling like it was sacrilegious to do anything other than some Christian activity during the first weeks following my surgeries. I listened only to Christian radio during that time. Instead of watching the news or sports on television, I felt like I should be praying and reading the Bible around the clock.

One day I found myself reading the Bible and realized when I looked up I couldn't remember a thing I had just read. My eyes were in motion, but my brain wasn't in gear. I had to be honest with myself and admit that, at the time, I just couldn't concentrate. So I laid my Bible aside, and that was okay. I knew in my heart God wasn't expecting me to read the Bible twenty-four hours a day just because I had cancer; nor would it impress Him in the least if I could do that.

And in those moments, I experienced anew just how great His love and grace are toward me in Christ. When I was totally helpless and there was simply nothing I could do to merit His favor, I realized again that He already loved me and, according to Matthew 7:11, His heart's desire was to provide good things. He was in control.

So I passed the time with one of my favorite activities: watching old movies. Some of the new videos are so vulgar that I can't watch them, but I still am an avid fan of the Pink Panther movies with Peter Sellers. I believe I could laugh at him if I were sitting on an operating table. I know his slapstick kind of comedy is not amusing to some but, to me, he's very funny. So I watched old movies and laughed until my sides hurt! But I think laughing helps. We know that it releases endorphins in the body that actually help you to feel better.

Here's the way Solomon put it in the book of Proverbs. *"A joyful heart makes a cheerful face, but when the heart is sad, the spirit is broken. . . .All the days of the afflicted are bad, but a cheerful heart has a continual feast"* (Proverbs 15:13, 15).

Another thing that helped to balance the anxiety for us was to have good friends, like Dean and Bertie Webb, with whom Judy and I could laugh. They are wonderful people who always have a smile. Bertie has since died of breast cancer, but even in the midst of her battle we were able to make jokes back and forth that others probably couldn't appreciate. I know people can't be laughing all the time in the midst of critical health situations, but laughing every once in a while surely can lighten the load, keep things in perspective, and relieve built-up tension.

BENEFITS OF TAKING TIME OUT

Taking time out from the blitz of shock, emotional upheaval, and onslaught of medical jargon will afford you great benefits. I understand that you may find yourself in an urgent situation in which immediate decisions must be made; but, if at all possible, allowing time to pass will help you to thoroughly understand and process all that you are facing.

Return to the Basics

Taking time out from all the commotion surrounding a serious illness allows time for the dust to settle, so to speak, and the priorities in life begin to come into view again. As I shared earlier in the book, one of the basics I returned to in my life was the underpinnings of my Christian faith.

I said to myself, *Okay, so I've got cancer. Does that mean God hates me? Does that mean God doesn't care what's happening to me? Am I really sure I'm a Christian? Does getting the cancer mean that I'm out of God's will? I don't think so.*

Those are tough questions, but I found that a life-and-death illness opens a whole gamut of questions, bar none. So I went through an honest questioning process. I suspect most people do, even though they may not feel free to talk about some of the tougher questions they ponder.

The good news is that by stepping back to the basics, I became convinced of the integrity of my faith. I am just as convinced of my salvation today as I ever have been. God didn't forget me. He's still with me. Cancer is not an eternal thing; God's salvation is. Cancer only exists in this lifetime as a physical ailment in the very fragile *space suit* of a body God has given me.

One of the basics I had to return to was facing my own mortality. Unless the Lord returns first, one day this body of mine is going to give way to physical death. The same is true for you. I'm facing this possibility at age 57 and, of course, that seems too soon for me to deal with it. But I would have to face the same issue if I were 87. Accepting this fact helps me to keep bitterness or self-pity from setting up in my heart. I'm not being short-changed by God. As a matter of fact, He's been incredibly generous with me. I'll just have to rest, knowing that the number of my days are in His hands—not mine.

Facing death as a fact of life also helps the reality of eternal life through Jesus Christ to come into clear focus. Sometimes people don't prepare for eternity because they deny or ignore their mortality. The truth is, physical death is not the end of life; it's just the end of life here on this earth and the launching pad for the fullness of eternal life in the presence of our Savior, Jesus Christ.

I absolutely believe that to be absent from the body is to be present with the Lord. My mortal body may sleep awaiting the resurrection, but my spirit will be instantaneously transported into the presence of the Lord when I die. That reality helped to free my mind a lot and bring my fear back under control.

When I pray I just let my mind dwell on the glories of eternal life, because in that life I won't have cancer; my shoulder and side won't hurt. I'll have a supernatural body that will never know suffering. Here's the way the apostle Paul put it: *"For our citizenship is in heaven, from which also we eagerly wait for a Savior, the Lord Jesus Christ; who will transform the body of our humble state into conformity with the body of His glory, by the exertion of the power that He has even to subject all things to Himself"* (Philippians 3:20–21).

I found that in order for me to get away and free my mind a little I had to go where I felt most comfortable. Everybody's got a favorite spot where they can retreat and feel most comfortable. For some people, it's lying in the bed. For others, it's sitting in a particular chair in a certain room. For others, it's walking in the cool night air. Whatever the case for you, find a spot where you can get away from the phone, visitors, and even family for a while—where you can think, pray, and process all that you're facing. My favorite place is upstairs in my study, sitting in my big old recliner chair.

It was interesting that events which were occurring all around me dimmed in terms of their significance during this time. It did not make any difference at that moment whether we were feeding the Bosnians. That would have been a matter of some concern to me previously. But when you pare your life back to the basics, I mean the essentials, nothing else matters. Only the Lord, my family, and the ministry God called me to were important.

Rely on Others

Taking time out to analyze your situation also provides the opportunity for you to rely on other people, especially if you're thrust into unfamiliar territory, such as a major medical problem. Relying on others didn't come easily to me—it never has—because I generally like to be in charge and provide for myself.

That doesn't mean that I actually want to do everything for myself, but I want to know all of my options and be able to make reasonably informed decisions. It was really frustrating to have the doctors continually talking in "medical-ese" rather than plain English.

Following my cancer diagnosis, however, all that changed. Many of the decisions I faced were beyond my ability to comprehend. Not only could I not comprehend all the medical data involved in making some decisions, I was not able to concentrate as I normally would. How was I supposed to make a major decision about metastatic kidney cancer when, in fact, I didn't even know what it was a short time before?

So I *had* to rely on other people. I began by calling friends in medicine and asking their advice. Fortunately, I happened to know a lot of doctors and was able to become reasonably informed rather quickly. You may not have access to doctors who are also personal friends. But do the best you can, and certainly seek out a second, or even third, opinion. Try to find a doctor who is willing to interpret the medical terms so you will know what you're up against. At the very least, buy a good guide to medical terminology.

Relinquish Matters Beyond Your Control

The more time I had to think clearly, the more I began to relinquish matters that really didn't directly affect my medical condition. The key was, until I came to the point of giving things totally to the Lord, they were a burden and a worry to me.

For instance, although I wasn't in the position of owning my own business, I did have the ministry to think about. It was a matter of no little concern to me how my health—and potentially my own death—would impact the future of CFC. But I had to give the responsibility for this over to God, who called the ministry into being in the first place, and simply put that concern out of my mind.

The point is, I needed to think other things through and believe that the Lord knew about the ministry's need; and He did. Allen, my oldest son, stepped up to provide leadership and stability for the organization during that time and did a fine job. I'm confident he will carry on—not in my steps per se but following God's leadership in his life as well. The key to real peace was that I knew I could count on God to provide the leadership the ministry would need if I left—either temporarily or permanently.

A similar concern was my responsibility for the CFC radio programs. I usually did the thirty-minute, call-in "Money Matters" program live every day. What would happen when I wasn't there? It was a live radio talk program that virtually nobody else could do—or at least that's what I thought.

In addition, I regularly taped our five-minute "How To Manage Your Money" programs. Although we didn't do that every day, it did have to continue during the time I was out. None of us wanted to air reruns, which become stale very quickly.

God already had an answer for this concern. We have really bright, creative people in our radio department. Under the leadership of Steve Moore, my co-host, our staff interviewed people all over the country on a daily basis, on a number of financial topics, and it all went very well. As well as we have been able to tell, we didn't lose any audience at all. In fact, I received a couple of letters from radio stations who liked the new format *better.*

God was faithful to me, our staff, and the ministry, just as you would expect. But again, my ability to relinquish these responsibilities, and truly have a peace about it, came with the passing of time. There was nothing to be gained by me sitting around and worrying about it. I couldn't have solved any of these problems. Worrying about them simply would have drained the energy and strength I needed to recuperate.

Another area I had to turn over to God was my concern over the speaking engagements I had booked for the remainder of the year. Some of these commitments had been made years before. Backing out of them would prove expensive for the host groups, considering the money spent on publicity and brochures. What would happen to their conferences? What would they think?

Again, with the benefit of time to temper my perspective, God helped me to see that He would supply other speakers for these events. They would take place and be successful whether I was there or not. In truth, I discovered that it was not only my concern for the organizations that heightened my anxiety but concern for my pride as well. I caught myself thinking, *"Well, if I'm not there, I won't ever have the opportunity to speak to that group again."* That may be true, but God's given me a peace about that also.

I truly believe the same principles apply to those of you who are seriously ill who also run your own businesses. Suppose you're an insurance agent who's self-employed. Of course, if you're not working, you're not generating an income. If you don't survive your illness, your family may be in tough financial straits. If there is something you can do about that in the immediate future, of course you should do it. If you can arrange for someone to oversee the business or help your spouse to keep it going, then get that done.

But don't worry about things that are beyond your control. Stop worrying about the things you can't change and concentrate on getting well. I just had to tell myself that over and over again. *"Don't worry about it."* That's a hard task for someone with my personality, but I just had to keep a clear perspective of the things I could control and yield to God the things I couldn't. With the passing of time, the distinction between those two areas became more apparent, and God's peace was multiplied in me as a result.

Another area I needed to yield control over was my commitment to exercise. To this day I'm limited as to how much I can do, both by the pain and physical limitations, as a result of the surgeries. There's no need for me to worry about it, however, since there is very little I can do to change the situation. Instead, I try to do what I *can*. In the past, I've been an avid exerciser, especially since I had my heart attack several years ago. I realize how important exercise is to maintaining a healthy body.

But my situation has obviously changed, and I can no longer do the things I used to do. I could worry and fret about it, but it wouldn't change the situation. So if I get up one day and feel good, I try to walk a mile or so. After that I usually hurt the following day, and so I don't exercise until the pain subsides. That's fine.

Some people might lapse into being a couch potato in their laziness because they really didn't want to exercise in the first place. But they probably were looking for excuses to quit anyway. My nature is the opposite. I was somewhat compulsive about my exercise, never missing a day. But that steadfast commitment to exercise is just another habit I've learned to modify to fit my new circumstances. I just have to be at peace with God about my overall health, including my new limitations.

I've also had to change my diet again, even though I didn't want to. After my heart attack, I never violated my dietary rules. It didn't matter if I was eating out with others or speaking at a banquet, I stuck to my low-fat diet. But after my cancer surgeries, I lost nearly thirty-five pounds—far more than I could afford to lose. Since I never have been one to gain weight easily, I had to change most of my dietary habits. I had to find the least fatty, high-calorie food available and eat a lot to regain my weight.

Part of this effort was complicated because my appetite disappeared after my surgeries. That's typical of how I react under stress: I just don't eat very much. Without much appetite I will go days with minimal food intake. So, I had to force myself to eat. Your problem may be just the opposite. If you're like Judy, you may eat more under stress. That's why no one plan fits all.

Talk about habit changes, I hadn't eaten a McDonald's hamburger in ten years, but when we were in Prague for the immune system therapy, the native food didn't agree with my system, and I made several trips to McDonalds—well, actually, many trips. Almost every day I ate a Big Mac. I probably hadn't eaten ten Big Macs in my whole life, but I had over forty of them while I was in Prague. I know fatty meats aren't good for my heart, but I had to gain some weight. My heart did fine, and now I eat vegetarian foods mostly, but the pizzas and Big Macs surely tasted good then.

Don't Worry About the Future

You may be in a situation in which you have several small children and, naturally, one big concern will always be, *How will my children make it without me?* Of course that preoccupies your mind because you love them. But God's not going to abandon them. Will your children face difficulties and sorrows in the time ahead? I'm sure they will. But isn't that true of life anyway?

You can't spend your time worrying about it because, in the end, you can't change it. If there is anything within your reasonable ability to do, then do it. If there is a close family member or relative you can place in charge of your children, then make those arrangements. Beyond that, don't worry about your children's college education or their future spouses or your future grandchildren.

In spite of our great parenting skills, God is an infinitely better parent and shepherd than we are, and He has promised He won't leave them (see John 14:18). Don't worry over whether your daughter can go to band camp next summer or how she will make it if you're not there for her. There's a time to be concerned with such issues but in the midst of a medical crisis is not the time. You need to get well, and worry retards that process, so just call a time-out.

"There is an appointed time for everything. And there is a time for every event under heaven—a time to give birth, and a time to die; a time to plant, and a time to uproot what is planted. A time to kill, and a time to heal; a time to tear down, and a time to build up. A time to weep, and a time to laugh; a time to mourn, and a time to dance. A time to throw stones, and a time to gather stones; a time to embrace, and a time to shun embracing. A time to search, and a time to give up as lost; a time to keep, and a time to throw away. A time to tear apart, and a time to sew together; a time to be silent, and a time to speak. A time to love, and a time to hate; a time for war, and a time for peace" (Ecclesiastes 3:1–8).

Take Time To Back Off

To accommodate the changes taking place with your health, you need to back off and change your priorities. Either you can fight change and be miserable, or you can go with the flow and enjoy to the fullest each day God provides. You don't have to control everything.

Take time to assess the changes taking place in your life. Identify the things you can make a difference in and relinquish the matters that are beyond your ability to control. You may discover you're not as essential to a great many matters as you think you are. That's what I discovered a long time ago.

In 1965 I was in charge of an experimental ground station on one of the manned space programs: Gemini. This position carried a great deal of responsibility, and to my surprise I got called for jury duty in Brevard County during launch week. My presence was considered absolutely critical to our part of the operation. So I obtained a letter from the head of NASA and the head of the Air Force Space Command, requesting that I be dismissed from the jury pool. I appeared in court early the following Monday morning, and when the judge asked if anyone had a reason to be excused I stepped forward with my credentials.

"What's your excuse?" the judge gruffed. He was a rotund man whose booming voice matched his physical size, and it was clear he had little sympathy for jury evaders.

I replied, "I have a letter from the heads of NASA and the Air Force at the Space Center. We have a launch coming up and my presence is absolutely essential for the mission."

I handed the letters to the bailiff who in turn handed them up to the judge, who was peering down from his raised position. The courtroom was dead quiet as His Honor reviewed the letters.

Finally, his eyes raised from the pages, and peering through his spectacles, he said, "Young man, let me ask you something."

"Yes sir," I responded.

"If you died today, would they cancel that launch?"

After considering his question I replied, "Well, no sir, I don't guess they would."

"Then you're not all that essential, are you?" And with that he handed me back the letters and motioned for me to take my place among the other prospective jurors. I have never forgotten that lesson: No one is really "essential."

As I shared earlier, I resigned as God's manager of the universe—a position to which I was never appointed anyway.

Taking time to face one's own mortality can really bring the essential issues of life into focus. Don't be afraid of time alone. Use it to commune with God and see things from His point of view.

CHAPTER THIRTEEN

✦

Cards and Letters

I believe God's people are the warmest and most compassionate people in the world, and I have included this section of the book as a testimony to that truth. Shortly after I announced the diagnosis of cancer on the radio, I began to receive cards and letters of encouragement from all over the world. I was deeply touched by the sentiments expressed by the writers and found great encouragement through their generosity.

Please know that Judy and I will always be grateful for each card, letter, and prayer offered on our behalf. I hesitated to include these messages in the book, knowing they could sound very self-serving. I only hope and trust that you will focus on the hearts and intentions of the writers as you read the letters and that you will experience God's love and encouragement the way I have through them.

But let me take these thoughts one step further. If you know people battling serious health conditions, why not drop them a card or letter? I had a great deal of attention because of my visibility to the public, but you may know others who are overlooked or suffering alone. Sow a word of kindness, hope, and encouragement if you know someone like that. God will bless that person just like I have been blessed, and you'll reap a blessing as well. Do it today.

The apostle Paul wrote, *"Blessed be the God and Father of our Lord Jesus Christ, the Father of mercies and God of all comfort; who comforts us in all our affliction so that we may be able to comfort those who are in any affliction with the comfort with which we ourselves are comforted by God"* (2 Corinthians 1:3–4).

SPECIAL NOTES AND CARDS FROM CHILDREN

Dear Mr. Burkett: I am so sorry in that you had cancer in your kidney and I am sorry that you still have it on your collar bone. I pray that God would help you with your daily expenses and I pray that the Lord would help you to keep on working in whatever you have to do.

Kathryn

Dear Mr. Burkett: I was very sorry to hear about your cancer. I know that God will always be faithful like He has in the past in providing all of your financial, physical, and spiritual needs. I pray that God will continue to heal you so that you can continue your business.

Michael

Dear Larry Burkett and family: Thank you for your ministry. Your faith is encouraging to me. I hope you get well soon. And I thank God that you are getting better. And I pray for your body as well as your ministry. Once again, thank you. I wish you well. God bless you. God loves you.

Gretchen, age 10

Dear Mr. Burkett: Hello! How have you been doing? I pray that our wonderful Lord will strengthen your body so you are able to continue your life and your radio broadcast. May He enable your body to not need any more operations, and may the enemy keep his hands off of you. May His continuous love and mercy keep you for the rest of your life.

Heidi, age 13

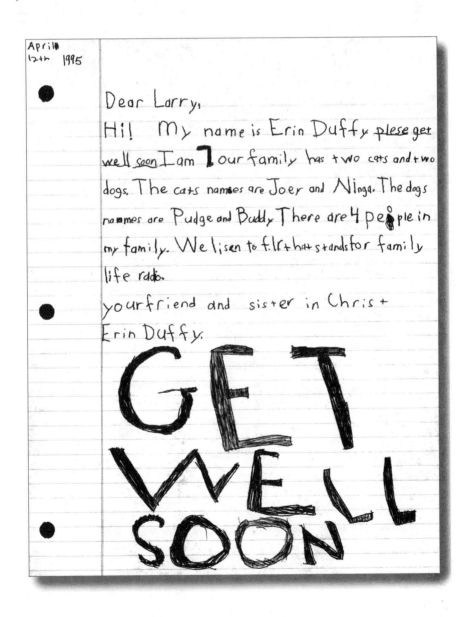

"I have set the LORD
    always before me.
Because He is at my
    right hand.
    I will not be
        shaken."
            Psalm 16:8

May 30, 1995

Dear Larry,

We are a family of 6 who live on a farm in north central Illinois.

We have been using your financial materials since 1988. You have helped us get out of debt. Financial freedom is _wonderful_! We praise God for you + your obedience.

GET WELL Soon!

Love,
RICK + Anne
Aaron, Mary,
Ruth + Wm
Campbell

(card drawn by Mary - age 13)
We're praying for you!

Larry —

I've been reading "Comeback" by Dave Dravecky, and at times during his fight against cancer he felt like giving up, but, he didn't. Keep pushing, Larry. I'm praying you'll soon be well.

your loving and faithful listener,

Sean Duffy

PS I'm 10 years old

Mr. Larry Burkett,

*M*ay God who hears our every prayer
restore good health to you,
and may the blessings of His love
be yours your whole life through.

Hope You're Feeling Better

"The Lord is my strength and my shield...."
PSALM 28:7

LETTERS/NOTES/CARDS FROM ADULTS

Dear Sir, I am writing from Switzerland. I listen to your program that comes to me by WVNE. Today I heard the dramatic news, about the two tumors. You did announce it with such a humble, submissive spirit, continuing to trust in your God, no matter what, that, should I not already be a believer in our Lord Jesus, listening to you this afternoon, I could have become one. You went on with the broadcast undisturbed, even occasionally laughing and seeing the reality of God in you. I am edified and I am sure many others are too.

I am praying for you and will do so with my Bible Study group. You have become a friend, a dear brother in the Lord. I also ask the Lord [to help me] to follow the example you gave me today for the rest of my life.

Helene

Dear Larry, Our prayers are with you as you recover from the difficult two surgeries you have undergone in the past few weeks. We are holding you and your family up to God—that His hands will touch all of you, bringing complete physical, mental and emotional healing of the scars caused by the cancer that was in your body. We pray that His peace would enfold you, lifting you above the pain, turmoil and anguish that you might otherwise be experiencing in these circumstances. You have been through a shock of gigantic proportions and no doubt are still reeling from the disbelief.

Larry, all we can suggest is that you rest on the prayers of others during this painful time, when your concentration and focus are weakened and you lack the power to pray for yourself due to your bewilderment. That's what the body of Christ is here to do— to hold up those who are hurting and wounded to the great God of peace and healing and mercy. We are praying for your healing every day during our quiet time together.

Bob and Patty

Dear Larry: Ten years ago the doctors found a rare tumor in my son's head. It was so big it encompassed every crevice of his brain and wrapped around the pituitary gland. The doctors said there was no hope for him to live. The Lord healed him and he is now a youth pastor at a local church. The Lord is no respecter of persons. He will do the same for you. I would like to pray for you (this way):

Father, your Word says in Matthew 18 "that if two of you agree on earth about anything that they may ask, it shall be done for them by My Father who is in heaven." Larry and I come to you in agreement today for Your perfect will in Larry's life. In the name of Jesus we bind Satan and every plan of destruction he has for Larry Burkett. Satan, you are trespassing on territory you have no right to touch. Larry Burkett is called, anointed, and chosen of God. The Lord has begun a good work in him, and He will complete it. We bind spirits of destruction, division, discouragement, disease, and death in Jesus' name. We loose life, restoration, unity, encouragement, perfect health and life in the name of our Lord Jesus Christ!

Father, I ask You to loose the angels to do warfare on Larry Burkett's behalf. I pray a hedge of protection over him and plead the blood of Jesus over Larry from the top of his head to the soles of his feet. I speak to every blood cell and bone cell and skin cell of his body to come in line with Your Word. We speak to his major organs to function as You have placed them in him to function. I thank You, Lord, that You have called Larry to preach the gospel, bring deliverance to the oppressed, and freedom to those held captive by Satan's devices.

Father, give his doctors wisdom as to what they should do. You said for us to do all we know to do and stand. We believe Your Word is true! We love You, Lord, and thank You for Jesus who died for our sins, who heals all our diseases and keeps our lives from destruction. Father, please bless Larry Burkett and his family financially, mentally, emotionally, physically, and spiritually, in Jesus' name. Amen!   Jenny

Dear Larry: Thank you for your ministry. It has been a blessing to my family and me. Your advice, from Bible-based principles, is a guiding light for people like myself. In a society of easy credit and increasing materialism, it would be easy to jump in that pool of major debt. Your great advice has helped me make decisions that have kept my family financial stress at low levels.

I am always impressed with the manner in which you address your callers [on the "Money Matters" radio call-in program]. It is obvious that you truly care about them. You're wonderful at doing the Lord's work.

My heart went out to you and your family as soon as I heard about your health condition. My family and I are keeping you in our prayers.

Jacobson family

Gracious Heavenly Father, I am committing myself as a prayer warrior for Larry Burkett during this time of special need of love and prayers. I do not know Larry except through what I have learned of him the year or so of listening to the radio and feeling that he is so in love with You, dear Lord.

When I first heard of his trouble this week, like so many, I asked "Why, Lord?" At my age, Lord, that question should not have entered my mind. You know me and how weak I am; I do know my strength is from You and You only. Holding Larry up to You is what I can do for him, and thank you Lord for the privilege I have of being able to hold special needs up to you. Lord, I am asking You for a *special, special* blessing for Larry and his family.

Another thing, Lord—not just an afterthought—please be in that operating room and give the doctors and attendants the mind and steady hands to be able to glorify You. This is in Your hands, powerful Lord. We are leaning on your hands, Lord, for the out-come, and shall give you all the praise. Thank you for what you have planned for all of us. In Christ's name, Amen.

P.S. Mr. Burkett: After living eighty-seven years (5-2-95), I have learned God is our strength and hiding place. I have been alone since 1-13-79. God has been so good to me. My body and bones are showing my age. I do thank God for my mind and the ability to be an encourager to those in my church and neighbors. I broke a bone in my back on 6-2-92, and have not been able to attend church. I do thank God for using me the way He is, and will keep you in my prayers.

Nancy

Dear Larry: I am a teacher in a small town on the Mississippi River in southeast Iowa. Yesterday, as I got in my van to drive home, I had on the Moody station out of Moline, Illinois. You were speaking right then about the tumors that have been found in your body, and asking for prayer from your listeners. I wanted to write you and let you know how important you have been to our family, and that we surely will be praying for you . . .

It may seem strange to write all this to you, but I wanted you to know how important your ministry has been to our family. [My husband] Joel never had a father to speak of. Our church back home lacked older male leadership. It seems that Joel has rarely had any mentor or more mature man to go to for advice. I believe you have filled a place in his life. I often thought that *if he had cancer, and the Make-A-Wish Foundation offered to let him meet anyone he wanted, that Joel would choose to visit your ministry and talk with you.* (emphasis added)

You can be assured that our family will be praying for you and your wife and children, as well as your ministry while you are distracted. We obviously feel that your time is not up yet. We will be believing for a complete healing—that it will be as though nothing was ever there. We look forward to many more years of you on the radio and in print.

Amelia

Dear Larry: I am delighted to hear your surgeries have been successful. With God's healing hand upon you, I pray that you'll be back in the studio in a matter of weeks. As a faithful listener to

"Money Matters" for the last two years, I can sincerely say I have missed you this last month and have prayed for you.

Do you realize, Larry, the tremendous impact on thousands of peoples' financial situations the Lord has allowed you to have? Your current involvement as the president and founder of CFC ministries is a classic example of someone who has fully opened his life to Christ's calling. You knew you had a national interest and ability to understand personal and business finances, and you simply said to the Lord, "If I can be used by You to help God's people to get a handle on their money troubles and to be better stewards of Your abundant resources, I am available and ready to head up that ministry."

Now all of these years later, look at what God has done through CFC! He is to be praised, indeed! Thank you for your ministry, your selfless devotion of your time and knowledge, and your commitment to base all your advice and decisions on God's principles as outlined in the Bible. There is none other who has taught these principles as clearly to me as you have over the last two years. You helped a great deal. It's true that all we have belongs to God. We are the caretakers. My husband and I are in our first year of marriage. We are *completely debt-free*. We set money aside regularly for retirement years; we are tithing on our gross incomes; and we are currently saving up for a down payment on a house in a year or so. We sense God's blessing on us, and are praying He'll provide for our needs when we have children and go down to only one income.

We listen with attentive ears and hearts to your sound Christian advice, Larry. Thanks again!

P.S. Judy, take good care of Larry and give him a hug for me, OK?

Elizabeth

Dear Larry: I have just learned of your illness and, along with thousands of those who have been assisted and ministered to by your work, I wanted to let you know that you will be in my prayers regularly. Over many years I have appreciated and enjoyed your Biblical commentary and direction in financial and other spiritual areas.

While I have been blessed to have a very financially responsible and conservative husband, who modeled personal financial accountability to our three, now adult, children, you have provided a wealth of confirming principles to undergird my own views. You have also provided me many thought-provoking ideas in areas that I had not dwelled on.

Thank you for your ever-gracious but never-compromising call to personal accountability. You are one of only a few "voices crying in the wilderness" in our era of widespread lack of understanding or interest in the honor of standing on ones' own financial feet, working hard and willingly sacrificing the short-term desires to accomplish long-term security.

Though God must be the source of all our security, He has given us intelligence, free wills, and the ability to reign in our "wants" in order to responsibly care for our "needs." You have tirelessly championed His wisdom from His Word, available to all of us. I thank you for your commitment to enlightening all people on this important area of our daily lives.

Larry, your life has enriched so many others. While you could have, with your abilities, become wealthy in earthly terms, you have chosen the better path and will certainly hear our Heavenly Father say, "Well done, good and faithful servant." I am confident that, until we all meet in eternity, you will never know how many lives you have touched for good.

It is my prayer that you will experience a full return to health and that God will continue to bless your ministry to His people at this juncture in time. Thousands of fellow Christians will be lifting you up in their prayers.

Joan

Mr. Burkett: I want to express my sincerest gratitude for your godly ministry. I have read a number of your books and listened to countless "sound-bytes" on the radio to find that you have a strong ministry to the world. There is no doubt in my mind that you have been called and gifted by God to minister to the world in the area of Bible-based finances.

I wanted to send you this letter to encourage you to keep up the good fight! God is not through using you yet. Stay very close to Him so the devil will not be able to bring your ministry down in any way. My wife and I want you to know that you will continue to be in our prayers, and we hope that someday we will be able to meet you to show our appreciation in person. Thanks again.

David and Amy

Dear Mr. Burkett: Even though letter writing is difficult for me, I felt an urgency to write you and your family. We were sorry to hear of your health problems and we are praying for God's hand to move in a mighty way in your life through these difficult times.

God has used you greatly and we are certain He will continue to do so. Thanks for your help. This year, for our son's Christian birthday, we bought your book called *The THOR Conspiracy.* At twelve, he read it in one day. Keep in mind that we teach him at home, so he did have some extra time to read it.

Although we don't know you or your wife, we wish to thank her also because we truly believe that the two are one and that her reward for sharing you with us will be equal. We wish to let her know that we are praying for her as well. We have gone through these things and sometimes the stress is harder on the one closest to you.

I hope this brings joy to your heart. May God's grace be all sufficient in this time of trouble.

Roger

Dear Larry: Our prayers are with you. So glad to hear things look excellent for you. I prayed that God wouldn't take you yet—the Christian and secular world desperately need your biblical wisdom on finances. You have helped so many people, our family included.

Thank you so much for heeding God's calling on your life. When God does call you, I know your crown will be filled with many jewels because you helped so many people. Thanks again!

Mary

Dear Larry: I am *so thankful* for you. You are a special blessing in my life, ever since the first time I heard you on the radio years ago. When I heard your testimony on the radio today, I was encouraged by the strength of your faith.

I finished treatments at M.D. Anderson this year for stage three type four breast cancer. I have children fifteen and thirteen. I am disease free as of my last check-up, but I too, realize we will all die. I was so upset about you having cancer, but strangely, God used it to comfort me, because you are such a faithful servant. I pray with all my heart that God restores your health and blesses you with a long life—see Psalm 41:1–3. I love you and I am your friend.

Judy

Mr. Burkett: We wanted you to know that we will be thinking of you and praying for you during this time of illness. God does answer prayers. My mother-in-law had throat cancer and after three doctors told her she would lose her voice, and have to have chemotherapy and radiation, the fourth doctor said he could get the cancer without losing her voice. That's been about six years ago now. There's been no further sign of the cancer and there was no chemotherapy or radiation therapy. We thank and praise God for this.

We know God will be with you and your family during this time. We pray that God will give you the peace that passes all understanding. Thank you again for allowing God to use you to bless us.

Mike and Mary Lou

Dear Larry: I am an attorney in the state of Minnesota. Prior to accepting Christ, money was my foremost concern.

In November of 1991, I was "channel surfing" and caught the last few minutes of a program dealing with monetary concerns. Being consumed with anything having to do with money, I naturally started paying attention. Toward the very end of the program, you were shown pointing out a Bible verse about charging interest. The verse, Deuteronomy 23:20, discussed charging a foreigner interest, but not a brother.

Initially I dismissed this as another one of those religious nuts trying to influence government policy. Forgive me if that sounds harsh, but that is actually what I said at the time. However, a few days later, I was still mulling this concept over and decided that if it bothered me that much, I should do something about it.

I set out to write a brief supporting my theory that religious zealots should not be allowed to have any say in our nation's fiscal policy. Standard procedure dictates to check out your opponent's arguments for strengths and weaknesses. So, I literally blew the dust off my Bible and dug in. Several of the verses I found made sense. As I kept digging, my interest in prophecy grew. I started comparing past events and recent headlines to various verses. A definite trend was beginning to form. Needless to say, my rabid fiscal arguments were put on the back burner. The more I discovered about prophecy and world events, the more uncomfortable and fearful I became.

On February 25, 1992, I accepted Jesus Christ as my lord and savior. Larry, this all started when the Holy Spirit used your ministry to "light my fuse." I thank God for the sacrifice He made for all of us on the cross. I also thank Him for your ministry. I'll continue to lift you in prayer for your recovery from your illness. It is my sincere hope that this letter brings a little happiness to you in knowing that the Lord has used your ministry in helping me to know Him as never before.

John

Dear Larry (and staff): We have enjoyed your newsletter and radio program and tapes through the years. We were greatly distressed to hear of your illness. Dr. James Dobson mentioned one of the dates of your operation and I awoke very early that morning and I am sure joined *many, many* people in prayer for you. Satan is truly after our leaders. You've meant a lot to us and you are in our prayers.

Susan and Wayne

Dear Larry: It touched my heart when I heard on the radio, while driving to work one morning, about your illness. Tears came to my eyes and I just kept asking the Lord, why did He allow this to happen to you?

Here I am doing just a nine-to-five job; and there you are serving the Lord in what He has called you to do—building up and strengthening the body of Christ. Why didn't He allow me to have cancer and let you go on serving Him? You are doing more good than I am! I thank God that you are a humble, godly servant. *If I could, I would gladly take your illness and let you go on serving Christ.* [italics added] The world needs men like you!

Charles

Dear Mr. Burkett: I am praying for continued healing during your post-operative therapy, and want to offer my personal encouragement to you during this new experience in your life. In August, 1990, I had my right shoulder blade removed, along with most of the shoulder socket. I have done real well even though I have limited movement of my right arm.

I know you have tremendous faith in our Lord. He will give you the strength to overcome any anxiety you may feel about the loss of your kidney and shoulder blade. If you get discouraged, please think of me and how I have no trouble driving my car, carrying groceries, attending college full-time . . . all the normal things in life. God will give you the ability to adjust just as He did me. So be encouraged, my brother in Christ! You give so much to us and God will make sure you continue to do that. My family is being blessed by your financial advice. We are giving more and more to the Lord as we pay off our huge stack of credit cards. Thank you so very much for your wonderful books and much needed advice. God bless you!

Walter

Dear Mr. Burkett: I wanted to let you know how your faith, and the way you have conducted yourself through this crisis, have helped me with my own walk with God. I hope if I ever go through something like you are going through, that I will be able to keep my faith as strong and be able to help others like you have done! I will never forget the day on the radio that you told us about your cancer. What a testimony for God! God bless you and your family!

Cindy

Dear Larry and family: You are in our prayers today! Karen and I are home from Africa to attend our daughter's wedding and we heard you are suffering with cancer. God is able! Three weeks before this photo was taken (photo enclosed of Swanee and Karen), Karen had double, radical mastectomy. Today she is strong and ever faithful in service.

Larry, *I knew* I had been successful in teaching my kids biblical economic principles when at Christmas time, one of my girls gave me one of your books! She liked it and said, "Dad, this man thinks just like you taught us."

Swanee

Dear Larry: We have wanted for some time to write you a note to share our concern, love and prayers with you. We are very grateful for your obedience to God and all we are learning from your ministry.

Gil and I have been married thirty-four years, starting out as dairy farmers. We then had a wood business and now he builds colonial tool sheds. It is only the last three years we have learned about proper finances. It took thirty-two years but we are out of debt and hope to stay that way by the grace of God (and our obedience).

I personally wanted to write and encourage you because eight years ago I lost my right kidney to a tumor. At the time of surgery, they prepared my husband and me because it had all the signs of being malignant. Fifteen days later, the doctor came in and said they could find no sign of cancer. Needless to say, we were very grateful to God. It was a time that changed my life and my walk with the Lord, bringing me into a deeper, closer relationship with Him. We know it is not what happens to us in life that matters, but our response to a holy God who definitely is in charge and knows what is best for us.

Gil and Charline

Dear Larry: I just heard about your surgery for cancer and wanted you to know that FCA is praying for you. You've touched many lives in the name of Jesus Christ and we want you to know that there are thousands who care for you. Please know that the Fellowship of Christian Athletes staff and volunteers have been alerted to pray for you in the upcoming surgery Monday and the recovery process.

Dal Shealy
President/CEO
Fellowship of Christian Athletes

Dear Larry: I always look forward to hearing your programs on the radio. You have been my motivation to finally become debt free. For that, I now have a bigger debt—a debt of gratitude.

I first heard of your cancer while I was driving down the road. I pulled to the side shoulder and wept and prayed for you. I knew God would hear all the prayers and respond positively, as He has. I will continue to pray for you and your wonderful ministry— see Galatians 6:9!

Julia

Dear Larry: Hearing your announcement over the radio yester-day of the discovery of two tumors, I went through a whole range of emotions. Because I am a registered nurse, I understand the possibilities that accompany such a diagnosis. I was very sad-dened. Then, as your testimony progressed, I was joyful!

Over the years, I have appreciated you and your labor for the Lord, not having met you, but appreciating you because of your stand for God, your love for Him, and your trust in Him.

I, my family, and our church will continue to pray that God's will be done in your life and that your faith will remain stead-fast—praying for your family as well!

Sara

Dear Larry: My husband and I are very sorry to hear about your trial of illnesses, the heart problems, and now the cancer. We have been praying continually for you and your ministry for the last two years when our Christian radio station started carrying your program, and especially more since we heard about your cancer. I know that you're a Christian, and you're not afraid to die, but I wanted to tell you, ever since I heard the news, I have felt that this illness God will use to further your ministry. I don't believe that this cancer is going to be something you will die from in the near future, if at all. I feel certain of this. God has blessed your ministry and He has blessed my husband and I because of the principles you have taught us.

So many people have been and are continually blessed because of your ministry. I believe Satan knows you indeed are a threat to him and that is why you have been a target lately, but Christian people I know are already praying for healing and the miracle of showing the world what God is continuing to do through you. I truly believe that you will be healed and your ministry increased.

I am a nurse for twenty-plus years, and I have seen the Lord take people home when I thought they were better, and I've seen people in comas, with no hope of recovery, get up and walk out of the hospital, telling me what I talked to them about while they were in a coma! So what I have learned is that no matter what the circumstances appear like, only God knows.

I do believe God will perform a miracle with you. We will continue to pray.

Mike and Dorothy

Dear Larry: I find it hard to understand why one who does so much good and is so needed to help so many people would have a trial like cancer to have to go through. But for sure, God never said we would get all the answers on all the issues on life situations—just that we trust Him through all of them.

I couldn't understand ten years ago when I myself had a mastectomy due to breast cancer. Mother of two young children, teaching Sunday School, working in mission work among many other facets. I just couldn't figure this interruption with this ordeal in my life. I had no time for cancer.

However, as I read in your newsletter that your ministry was really God's, not yours, it reminded me how God can use a tragedy or illness in our lives to further His work. The only things that come in our lives not sent directly by God are the ones He just allowed to come. He knows when every baby sparrow falls to the ground and I know His eye watches me and you.

I've prayed for you and will continue to do so.

Jackie

My dear Larry: Warm affection in Christ and assurances of special prayer for you. . . . I trust that by this time, you are receiving a favorable report from your doctors. We are looking forward to your return to the States [written while the Burketts were in Prague] and full and speedy recovery, that God will use this experience of cancer to draw you closer to His great loving heart and give you an even more urgent message to encourage people to receive the free gift of God's grace and the Lord Jesus.

Bill Bright
Campus Crusade for Christ International

[A copy of a fax from Dr. Bill Bright to Dr. David Yonggi Cho of the Yoido Full Gospel Church in Seoul, South Korea]

My dear Dr. Cho, beloved friend: Warm greetings and love from Orlando, Florida. A very dear and special friend, Dr. Larry Burkett, an outstanding leader in America has just learned that he has cancer. He has asked me to contact you to request your prayers and the prayers of your people for his healing. Thank you for honoring his request.

[The reply from Dr. Cho]

Thank you for your fax prayer request from your friend, Dr. Larry Burkett, who has cancer. Your fax came yesterday but due to Dr. Cho's heavy schedule, he did not return to the office all day; however, he will be in the office this afternoon after he has preached the third service and he will receive your request for prayer. After he prays, we will send your fax to prayer mountain for more prayer. Please be assured that Dr. Cho will pray for Dr. Burkett, as well as a host of believers at prayer mountain!

* * * * *

Due to the ties between radio stations and our CFC radio department, some correspondence came directly to the attention of Steve Moore, Vice President, Broadcasting. The following two letters are representative of dozens of others.

Dear Mr. Moore: Many thanks for your recent note about Larry Burkett. We appreciate the update and are grateful to God for his good progress. My boss was out for surgery at Christmas time and what an impact on our organization! Everyone's day got longer. Responsibilities were scrambled and shifted the best we could. So I know the stress and grief that go along with health problems inside an organization. Though Mr. Burkett humbly says Christian Financial Concepts is not built around one man, we want to extend our prayers and best wishes to that one man for his vision and so many years of sparkling Christian programming. Please know the entire CFC team is especially now remembered in prayer during our morning staff worship. God bless each one.

Dawn Hibbard, Program Director of Good News Radio

Dear Steve: We have received your letter concerning Larry's health. We were surprised to hear of that situation, but please know that we are standing with you in prayer for this man of God. My only sister, who was not saved, found out she had breast cancer. She went through three years of treatments and surgery, having both breasts removed. In December, shortly before Christmas, she was told she had a month to live. About two days later, the doctors were shocked to discover that the cancer was gone. In January, she accepted Christ, admitting that only He could have healed her. The cancer came back, and she kept the faith. At the hospital, she prayed for and witnessed to the doctors, nurses, patients, and even the chaplain! Her cancer was again healed!

The purpose of this testimony is to give a witness to the fact that sometimes God waits to move at the seemingly most critical time. But He does move. We'll continue to pray and hope that you guys continue to give us updates. God bless all of you, and thanks for your ministry.

Joey F. Langlinais, Program Director of KSJY

Recommended
Reading List

(This list is provided for the reader's interest only. The authors of this book do not necessarily endorse any information, advice, or counsel given in the following publications or by the organizations represented.)

Alternative Health Care Resources, Brett Jason Sinclair (Parker Publishing: West Nyack, New York).

Alternative Medicine Digest, 1-800-818-6777.

An Alternative Medicine Definitive Guide to Cancer: Breaking Through the Cancer Puzzle, W. John Diamond, Nathaniel Mead, and Burton Goldberg (Future Medicine Publishing: Puyallup, Washington).

Alternative Medicine: The Definitive Guide (Future Medicine Publishing: Puyallup, Washington).

Alternative Medicine Yellow Pages (Future Medicine Publishing: Puyallup, Washington).

Betrayal of Health: The Impact of Nutrition, Environment, and Lifestyle on Illness in America, Joseph Beasley (Random House: New York).

Body Reflexology: Healing at Your Fingertips, Mildred Carter, Tammy Weber (Parker Publishing: West Nyack, New York).

The Book of Raw Fruit and Vegetable Juices and Drinks, William H. Lee (Keats Publishing: New Canaan, Connecticut).

Burton Goldberg Presents an Alternative Medicine Definitive Guide to Cancer, W. John Diamond, M.D. and W. Lee Cowden, M.D. with Burton Goldberg (Future Medicine Publishing, Inc.: Tiburon, California).

Cancer: A Healing Crisis, Jack Tropp (Exposition Press: Smithtown, New York).

Cancer and Its Nutritional Therapies, Richard A. Passwater (Keats Publishing: New Canaan, Connecticut).

A Cancer Battle Plan, Anne E. Frahm with David J. Frahm (Piñon Press: Colorado Springs, Colorado).

The Cancer Industry: The Classic Exposé on the Cancer Establishment, Ralph Moss (Paragon).

The Cancer Microbe, Alan Cantwell Jr. (Aries Rising Press: Los Angeles, California).

Cancer Prevention and Its Nutritional Therapies, Rev. Edition, Richard Passwater (Keats Publishing: New Canaan, Connecticut).

A Cancer Therapy: Results of Fifty Cases, Max Gerson (The Gerson Institute in association with Station Hill Press, Inc.: Bonita, California).

Cancer Therapy: The Independent Consumer's Guide to Non-Toxic Treatment and Prevention, Ralph Moss (Equinox Press: New York).

Celebration of Healing: An Emily Gardiner Neal Reader, Emily Gardiner Neal (Cowley Publications: Boston, Massachusetts).

The Colon Health Handbook, Robert Gray (Rockridge Publishing: Oakland, California).

The Conquest of Cancer, Vaccines and Diet, Virginia Livingston-Wheeler, Edmond G. Addeo (Franklin Watts: New York).

The Cure for All Diseases, Hulda Regehr Clark (ProMotion Publishing: San Diego, California).

Dentistry Without Mercury, Sam Ziff, Michael F. Ziff (Bio-Probe, Inc.: Orlando, Florida).

Divided Legacy: The Conflict Between Homeopathy and the American Medical Association, Science and Ethics in American Medicine, Harris Coulter (North Atlantic: Berkeley, California).

Divided Legacy: A History of the Schism in Medical Thought, Vol. IV, Harris Coulter (North Atlantic: Berkeley, California).

Electro Pollution: How To Protect Yourself Against It, Roger Coghill (Thorsons Publishers Limited, Northamptonshire, England).

Encyclopedia of Natural Medicine, Michael Murray, Joseph Pizzorno (Prima Publishing: Rocklin, California).

Flax Oil As a True Aid Against Arthritis, Heart Infarction, Cancer and Other Diseases, Johanna Budwig (Apple Publishing: Vancouver, British Columbia, Canada).

Food—Your Miracle Medicine: How Food Can Prevent and Cure Over 100 Symptoms and Problems, Jean Carver (HarperCollins Publishers: New York).

Guess What Came to Dinner: Parasites and Your Health, Ann Louise Gittleman (Avery Publishing Group: Garden City Park, New York).

Healing with Whole Foods, Paul Pitchford (North Atlantic Books: Berkeley, California).

Hydrogen Peroxide: Medical Miracle, William Campbell Douglass (Second Opinion Publishing: Atlanta, Georgia).

Hypo-thyroidism: The Unsuspected Illness, Broda O. Barnes, Lawrence Galton (Harper & Row: New York).

Mucusless Diet Healing System, Arnold Ehret (Ehret Literature Publishing: Dobbs Ferry, New York).

Natural Healing with Herbs, Humbart Santillo (Holm Press: Prescott, Arizona).

Oxygen Multistep Therapy: Physiological and Technical Foundations, Manfred von Ardenne (Thieme Medical Publishers: New York).

Oxygen Therapies: A New Way of Approaching Disease, Ed McCabe (Energy Publications: Morrisville, New York).

Parasites, An Epidemic in Disguise, Stanley Weinberger (Larkspur, California).

Prevent Cancer Now, 2nd Ed., Michael Colgan (C.I. Publications: San Diego, California).

Racketeering in Medicine, J.P. Carter (Hampton Roads Publishing Company: Norfolk, Virginia).

Remove the Thorn and God Will Heal, Bud Curtis (Belco: Whittier, California).

Revolution in Technology, Medicine and Society, Conversion of Gravity Field Energy, Hans A. Nieper (Druckhaus Neve Stalling, Oldenburg, M.I.T. Management Interessengemeinschaft, Federal Republic of Germany).

Root Canal Cover-Up, George E. Meinig (Bion Publishing: Ojai, California).

Sharks Don't Get Cancer: How Shark Cartilage Could Save Your Life, I. William Lane (Avery Publishing: Garden City Park, New York).

Stress Without Distress, Hans Selye (Penguin Books: New York).

The Survival Factor in Neoplastic and Viral Diseases, William Frederick Koch (The Vanderkloot Press: Detroit, Michigan).

Third Opinion, Second Edition, John M. Fink (Avery Publishing Group: Garden City Park, New York).

Three Years of HCL Therapy, The Torrance Company (Portage, Michigan).

Toxic Terror: The Truth Behind the Cancer Scares, Elizabeth Whelan (Prometheus Books: Buffalo, New York).

Vitamin C Against Cancer, H.L. Newbold (Stein & Day Publishers: New York).

Water Fit To Drink, Carol Keough (Rodale Press: Emmaus, Pennsylvania).

When Cancer Comes: Mobilizing Physical, Emotional, and Spiritual Resources to Combat One of Life's Most Dreaded Diseases, Don Hawkins, Daniel L. Koppersmith, Ginger Koppersmith (Moody Press: Chicago, Illinois).

Winning the Fight Against Breast Cancer: The Nutritional Approach, Carlton Fredericks (Grosset & Dunlap: New York).

You Don't Have To Die, Harry M. Hoxsey (Milestone Books: New York).

PHONE NUMBERS AND ADDRESSES

For free publications about cancer and its treatments, call the National Cancer Institute at

(800) 4-CANCER.

NOTE: The Aliatros Clinic is no longer treating patients. However, the same treatment is now available in the U.S.

Contact: Biorem
PO Box 1295
Oakwood, GA 30566
(770) 967-8238

Christian Financial Concepts Inc.

Teaching | Biblical Principles of Managing Money

Larry Burkett, founder and president of Christian Financial Concepts, is the best-selling author of 49 books on business and personal finances and two novels. He also hosts two radio programs broadcast on hundreds of stations worldwide.

Larry earned B.S. degrees in marketing and in finance, and recently an Honorary Doctorate in Economics was conferred by Southwest Baptist University. For several years Larry served as a manager in the space program at Cape Canaveral, Florida. He also has been vice president of an electronics manufacturing firm. Larry's education, business experience, and solid understanding of God's Word enable him to give practical, Bible-based financial counsel to families, churches, and businesses.

Founded in 1976, Christian Financial Concepts, Inc. is a nonprofit, nondenominational ministry dedicated to helping God's people gain a clear understanding of how to manage their money according to scriptural principles. Although practical assistance is provided on many levels, the purpose of CFC is simply *to bring glory to God by freeing His people from financial bondage so they may serve Him to their utmost.*

One major avenue of ministry involves the training of volunteers in budget and debt counseling and linking them with financially troubled families and individuals through a nationwide referral network. CFC also provides financial management seminars and workshops for churches and other groups. (Formats available include audio, video, and live instruction.) A full line of printed and audio-visual materials related to money management is available through CFC's materials department (1-800-722-1976) or via the Internet (http://www.cfcministry.org).

Career Pathways, another outreach of Christian Financial Concepts, helps teenagers and adults find their occupational calling. The Career Pathways "assessment" gauges a person's work priorities, skills, vocational interests, and personality. Reports in each of these areas define a person's strengths, weaknesses, and unique, God-given pattern for work.

Visit CFC's Internet site at http://www.cfcministry.org or write to the address below for further information.

Christian Financial Concepts
PO Box 2458
Gainesville, GA 30503-2458

Editing:
Adeline Griffith
Christian Financial Concepts
Gainesville, Georgia

Text Design:
Ragont Design
Rolling Meadows, Illinois

Cover Design:
The Puckett Group
Atlanta, Georgia

Printing and Binding:
Quebecor Printing Martinsburg
Martinsburg, West Virginia

Moody Press, a ministry of Moody Bible Institute,
is designed for education, evangelization, and edification.
If we may assist you in knowing more about Christ
and the Christian life, please write us without obligation:
Moody Press, c/o MLM, Chicago, Illinois 60610.